DATE DUE

DISCARDED

Demco, Inc. 38-293

JAN 2 0 2012

THE WHITE COLLAR BOOK

Copyright © 2011 Bruce Meyer & Carolyn Meyer

Library and Archives Canada Cataloguing in Publication

The white collar book : poetry and prose of Canadian business life /
    edited by Bruce Meyer and Carolyn Meyer.

ISBN 978-0-88753-495-9

1. Working class--Literary collections. 2. Working class writings,
    Canadian (English). 3. Business--Literary collections. 4.
Labor--Literary   collections. 5. Canadian literature
(English)--21st century. I. Meyer, Bruce, 1957- II. Meyer, Carolyn
Margaret, 1962-

PS8235.W73W45 2011   C810.8'03553   C2011-905511-2

Design: Kate Hargreaves

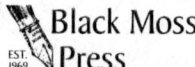

Published by Black Moss Press at 2450 Byng Road, Windsor, Ontario,
N8W 3E8 Canada. Black Moss books are distributed in Canada and
the U.S. by LitDistCo. All orders should be directed to LitDistCo.
Black Moss Press books can also be found on our website www.
blackmosspress.com.

Black Moss would like to acknowledge the generous financial support
from both the Canada Council for the Arts and the Ontario Arts
Council.

PRINTED IN CANADA

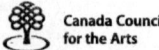 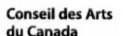 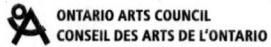

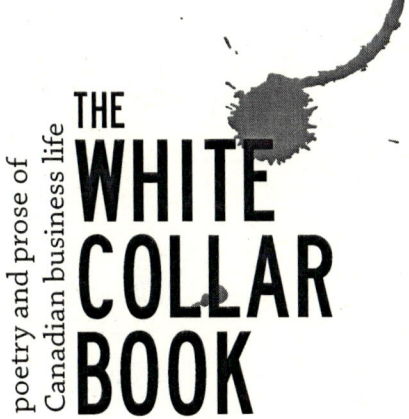

THE WHITE COLLAR BOOK

poetry and prose of Canadian business life

edited by
Bruce & Carolyn Meyer
foreword by Conrad Black

Black Moss Press
2011

To Margaret...who made us her business.

THE FILING SYSTEM

Conrad Black	• Foreword	8
Bruce & Carolyn Meyer	• Introduction	11
Martha Baillie	• *from The* Incident Report	22
Brian Bartlett	• Foot-Doctor for the Homeless	24
	• The Sonographer	27
Marilyn Bowering	• "Why are you here, my dear students?"	30
April Bulmer	• Office Supplies	31
Barry Callaghan	• Mellow Yellow	34
James Clarke	• Business Meeting	49
	• Entrpreneurial Discretion	51
Brian Campbell	• Pantoum of a Hired Man	52
Sue Chenette	• Why I Like My Car Heater	54
Brandon Crilly	• The Black Room	55
Cyril Dabydeen	• Conversation	61
Carlinda D'Alimonte	• Fissures	62
Christopher Doda	• A Sad Effect of Tenure	65
Paula Eisenstein	• Ships at Sea	67
Jesse Patrick Ferguson	• Push Pins Against Forgetting	71
	• What's His Face	73

Marty Gervais	• The White Shirt	75
Steven Heighton	• Noughts & Crosses	77
Bill Howell	• Management has Decided You May Prefer to Hear Something Else at this Time	97
A.M. Klein	• Annual Banquet: Chambre de Commerce	98
Stephen Leacock	• My Financial Career	100
John B. Lee	• Cruel With Books	105
Seymour Mayne	• For the Dentist Who Extracted My Last Wisdom Tooth	107
Bruce Meyer	• Death and the Human Resources Manager	108
	• Success	109
Shane Neilson	• No Ill Effects	110
John Oughton	• Ode to the TD Bank	112
P.K. Page	• The Stenographers	113
Molly Peacock	• Our Room	115
Lauralee Proudfoot	• Overload (A Rictameter)	116
Julie Roorda	• Words Misread on the Lips	118
Robert Service	• Five Per-Cent	120
Adam Sol	• City Song	122
Raymond Souster	• This Day	124
Robert Sward	• Millionaire	125

George Swede	• "windowless office"	129
	• A Local History of Hope	131
H. Masud Taj	• The Domain of Inbetween	132
Priscila Uppal	• A Referral	142
	• My Ovidian Education	143
	• My Stomach Files a Lawsuit	144
Halli Villegas	• The Path	147
Beverley Wicks	• Tunnels	167
Contributors		169
The Editors		188
Acknowledgements		190

FOREWORD

A collection of literary reflections on the workplace is such a brilliant and natural idea that I wonder why I haven't seen one before. So many authors, especially in the ages of the shopkeeper (Dickens), light industry (Steinbeck), the unionized industrial revolution (Upton Sinclair), have drawn on the work place that it rivals the boudoir, the palace or manor, the army and navy, and the demi-monde of criminals, revolutionaries, and police as a milieu for novels.

The Introduction mentions Sinclair Lewis and Theodore Dreiser, but a great many other and pre-twentieth century authors and authors in other cultures, such as Balzac, Proust, Zola, Flaubert, Chekhov, and Kafka could just as easily be cited. They were not as overt propagandists for the working class as Sinclair and Dreiser, but they hewed unforgettable novels from the timber of humble work.

And many profound authors passed some of their lives in the most implausibly mundane work. No matter how often one reads of it, it is hard to imagine T.S. Eliot, the fugitive from Missouri low church Protestantism, scrabbling out his livelihood and trying to support his young and neurotic wife, from his factotum's income from a small London publishing house. Just as it is hard to imagine the author of Wallace Stevens' fine verse driving around New England for decades selling insurance (quite successfully).

The anthologists in their Introduction credit novelists, poets, and film-makers as the conservators of the perspective and relevance of the individual, and the editors as the best people left at the barricades against the undifferentiated deluge of information and pap that floods in on us now. This carefully selected arrangement of prose and poetic workplace-related personality sketches and activity-descriptions gives a well-rounded perspective on a great range of work conditions, attitudes, and consequences. The sequence is a well-paced alternation of lengths, styles, and prose and poetry that builds subtly around its common element.

The work of thoughtful, elegant, and accomplished anthologists, and writers, this volume is a useful, provocative, and altogether pleasing read. I'm sure many readers will end as I began here, wondering why there are not already numerous compilations on this theme, as there are for sea stories, mysteries, sports epics, groups of literary contemporaries, short stories generally, and so on. And it is worth noting that this book and its theme lose nothing and add much by being confined to Canadian contributors.

This is a delightful volume, and it is a privilege to have been asked to contribute to it, however modestly.

Conrad Black
Miami, Florida, USA
October 18, 2011

INTRODUCTION

Business and professional life is the great unknown. Knowledge-work is often complex and complicated. It may require years of training to know how to do it competently and further training on the job to know how to do it up to employers' expectations. It is no easy task to understand what other people do for a living: only artists and writers, though, may know how to get under the skin of others enough to be able to make us suspend our disbelief about a work life that is not our own. Social scientists, especially ethnographic researchers, shadow and observe their business subjects—digging into their archived documents and emails, interviewing them intensively, and questioning them about the minutae of their daily routines—to get a take on what they do. Creative writers, on the other hand, are traditionally told from the beginning of their careers, to write about what they know. The 'otherness' of professional life, in all its complexities, therefore, becomes a less inviting subject.

A popular saying goes that while some work to live, others live to work. If work is an economic necessity, it is also a psychological imperative and, for some, a compulsive addiction. It keeps us sane. It drives us crazy. A curse, a duty, a blessing—sometimes all at once or each in quick succession in a single day—work is never short on ambiguities or paradoxes.

To be a professional is not only to do work but 'to speak for' what one does, to engage language both in the practice of tasks and in foreseeing and imagining the end results. We become our work but our work 'becomes' us. We are what we do, but we are more than the sum total of our job descriptions. W. H. Auden wrote of how it is possible for work to take us out of ourselves, to forget ourselves "in a function" (Horae Canonicae). Word knowledge—knowing how to do one's job—can bring self-knowledge, a sounding of one's potential. Our lives are defined, and sometimes ruled, by the professions we choose, the jobs we find (or which find us) and the rhythms and resonances of the work we carry out to earn a living.

According to Richard Florida, author of *Who's Your City?* the three most important decisions we'll ever make are choosing a life partner, choosing a place to live, and finding an "ideal" job—a job which in today's creative economy may be knowledge intensive beyond the mental and clerical work that typically defines a traditional white collar job. Finding the right job involves an important decision and is, therefore, something over which we have some measure of control…with any luck.

The commonplaceness of the job satisfaction survey suggests that in our work, regardless of how "ideal" the job is, our goal is happiness…or something like happiness. What we are meant to find is some level of fulfillment, self-actualization, and the peace of mind that comes from attaining society's definition of success, though this may be at odds with our personal definitions of success. A job that suits us holds the promise that work can be, in the words of Noel Coward, "much more fun than fun," but it is a goal that often falls short of reality.

At best, our work and the people we work with and for provides structure to our lives and the lives of others. In turn our actions and interactions support the structures and systems of a white collar world. White collar work involves problem-solving, something it shares with the making of literature. We may be dissatisfied to the point where we complain about our jobs—bitterly, cathartically, and even recreationally. The rarified world of the office, with its conflicts, political power plays, absurdities and boredom, is a ready target for satire because at the end of the day white collar work is about systems and structures and we feel a need to constantly reform them—to work better and smarter.

Finding ourselves without work we can all too soon discover what it gives back to us—not just an income or benefits—money, status and power—but a sense of purpose and belonging, the potential to make things happen, the elixir of identity and self-esteem, a place to be and become. In that 'becoming' we morph into our professional selves, the job titles on our business cards. We become dualistic beings, with our work personae at times radically at odds with who we feel we really are or want to be. The workplace is theatre. If we lose our jobs or leave them temporarily, we can easily lose ourselves, or at least a large part of who we are—the big fear of workaholics. We cease to exist as characters on our former stage.

Our parents and our grandparents—living through the deprivations of the Great Depression or uncertainties of immigration—knew all too well how holding a job held life in the balance. Work was and remains a means to survive and to strive. With the Great Recession of 2008 and the sobering realities of the current downturn of the global economy, we may struggle to find a job and, if lucky enough to get one and hold on to it, struggle again to find meaning in the routines and conventionalities of our work lives. Work can be exhausting, boring, and ennui-inducing, no matter how much enthusiasm we bring to the job each morning. With the advent of the mobile digital age, we are always connected, if not physically then virtually to our work and workplaces. As Naomi Baron has commented, we are "always on." The finite, nine-to-five workday has been forever banished. Our work is never done. The reality we face is a simple maxim: work—can live with it, can't live without it.

Globalization and the digital revolution have impacted how we do business, think of business and speak of business in every conceivable way. A fact of business today is that we do business within virtual communities and communities of discourse and discipline sometimes spanning the globe. We may never meet the people who communicate with us in solving problems and achieving goals. They are, to a certain degree, imaginary constructs. The professional world is now a conceptual world, so that our imaginations are taken up with the tasks before us, where the creation of products and the achievement of end-results involves a high degree of abstraction. We now live and work in an 'idea economy' with ever more stringent intellectual property laws to protect the fruits of our labours.

The connection between business—sometimes thought of as a numbers game—and language is a powerful one. The worldwide dominance of English, increased through globalization and international competition, owes a good deal to the need for a lingua franca, a common language that can be used to get work done. In many parts of the world, English is now the official corporate language, reborn as BELF —business English as a lingua franca—a language that is simple, clear, free of idioms and figurative constructions but still retaining business vocabulary and requiring proficient knowledge of the genres relevant to an individual's profession (Karkaaranta & Planken, 2010). We write on the job—an email, a letter, a report—but far less about the job. English becomes a universal language of business practice and protocol, with a serviceably restricted vocabulary and reach—enough to get by and get the job done in a given context. This can be at times at odds with the expansive nature of literary expression. On the one hand, there is an explosion in the use of English, while on the other hand English for business purposes is a far less rich language than what poetry and fiction tend to demand.

Much of workplace life is about fitting in—understanding what rules and norms operate, learning to behave, dress and even write like everyone else: being a "team-player." If you talk the talk, you fit in. If all of this were not clear enough already, there are corporate mission statements, codes of ethics, handbooks, directives from the top brass, reams of employment legislation, and the fine print in employment contracts—the proverbial confidentiality agreements and non-compete clauses—to prod and inspire us towards right conduct on the job. The pressures of conformity also have their drawbacks—witness the groupthink that can plague even the most innocuous business meeting—that thwart creative problem-solving and moments of inspiration. That's what 'thinking outside the box' is all about. Being in business often means being part of a collective or a profession—something larger than ourselves—and this inevitably presents challenges to our sense of individuality.

So why do so few writers today write about business and professional life? Is a person's workplace and work-life the last taboo of literature? Or is it just that we are too bored by it or inured to it that we have ceased to care and give it play in our imaginations?

While the workaday world looms large in popular entertainment—witness the recent bumper-crop of hit films and television shows including *Up in the*

Air, Swimming with Sharks, Horrible Bosses, The Messenger, The Office, Mad Men, to say nothing of the genres of the corporate law and medical dramas—it fails to exercise the same kind of hold on our literary imagination, or at least not to the extent that it once did. We can laugh or cry at seeing the absurdities and betrayals of our own work lives played out for us in these easily recognizable genres—the old standards of comedy, tragedy and didactics.

Judging from the nonfiction titles that business travelers grab at airport kiosks on their way to catch a red-eye, many of us dislike our jobs (and to a lesser extent our bosses and coworkers, along with the daily mundanities and rigid hierarchies). It may also be that we dislike the people we become or fear becoming through our work. The self-help-at-work sub-genre plays on our insecurities and perceived inadequacies and promises a quick fix for those who feel they ought to be better at what they do. For every business skill or process—networking, public speaking, chairing meetings—there are those ready, for a price, to tell us how to do it better or more productively. The cult of business/work has its own acolytes, gurus and mantras, all fodder for a publishing world that continues to churn out hubris-fuelled biographies, variations on the classic how-to-succeed-in-business primer, true confessions of business insiders, and cautionary tales of CEOs and their corporations gone wrong. Such stories also fill the gaps between prognostications and postmortems in daily business pages and mass-circulation business magazines. Taken together, these works reflect our collective obsession with business and professional matters, whether we love or loathe them. Even when we are not at work, we are still inhabiting our work world through its many narratives and genres. It is never far away.

While the Grisham-esque business thriller—with its ambition-and-intrigue-soaked plotlines played out by conspiratorial CEOs, greedy balance-sheet fraudsters, and righteous whistle-blowers on-the-run—has become an identifiable genre, there are relatively few serious writers of fiction and poetry who venture in any sustained way into the imaginative terrain of the corporate drama or who care to write about work other than their own. A hundred years after novelists such as Sinclair Lewis and Theodore Dreiser grappled with issues of business and the social consequences of capitalism in their fiction (and more than half a century after Mordecai Richler helped to adapt John Braine's *A Room at the Top* for the screen), the urge to write about business has, paradoxically, waned considerably in a world that is increasingly corporatized and in which human life can never be entirely untouched by business, commercial enterprise and consumer culture. Great business narratives—Ken Lay and the Enron scandal, the collapse of Nortel, the vicissitudes of Steve Jobs at the hands of the company he founded, the phone-hacking 'journalism' of Rupert Murdoch's *News of the World* editors—are headline grabbers that pass in and out of popular consciousness but help to reinforce perceptions of the corporate world as unjust and corrupt.

We live in an unfiltered world where information is no longer vetted through the purview of editors and publishers. Unparalleled, multi-channel media coverage and an abundance of social media now make it possible to know every detail of such events as they unfold and to participate in the ongoing public dialogue about them. The place of the creative writer in bringing these events into lens-like focus or in pointing out the human truths behind them is no longer a privileged one. Through tweets, blogs and Facebook comments, we can all weigh in as arbiters of these corporate dramas and add to the collective schadenfreude whenever big business finds itself in big trouble. The outline of these narratives of business and corporate life are ones we know by heart—archetypes as old as business, commerce and literature. We feed our appetite for such stories through a succession of media sources and outlets, each giving us more detail than the last until our interest in following the arc of the story wanes. In our online, op-ed world, though, fiction-writers, poets, and film-makers give us what we can get in no other way. They are the last line of resistance against the abdication of individuality and the last ones to believe that the bottom line they speak for is human truths.

C.M. & B.M.
August 2011

Martha Baillie
from THE INCIDENT REPORT

#5

In the library workroom, a schedule hangs from two clips. As always, the day has been divided into compartments, as if it were a train about to set out on a well-planned voyage along shining rails. My initials have been pencilled into many of the little boxes that correspond to each hour between 9 AM and 8:30 PM. We, the staff, don't always greet the public with enthusiasm. We don't feel, every one of us without fail, that we are travelling out, embarked upon an adventure, and yet there we are, inscribed in our little boxes, as if the day were pulled by a solid locomotive.

Every morning in the warmth of my bed, as I surface from sleep, fear—small as a cherry stone, it cracks open behind my breastbone. I don't want the fruit. With each quick breath the fear grows, a rustling of leaves in the cavity of my chest. But soon I've washed, dressed, drunk a cup of tea, eaten a piece of toast, and am on my way to work, riding my bicycle in a prescribed direction.

#8

According to yesterday's schedule, Wednesday, April 1, 2009, between the hours of ten and eleven, I was to do the Holds Alert Report. It fell to me to locate on our shelves, and send off to the correct destinations, the items listed as having been requested by patrons in other branches scattered across the city.

I wheeled my metal cart around the library, and for every book, DVD, CD or video I successfully found and pulled from the shelf, for every item neither stolen nor misshelved, I inscribed a thick red check mark on the list. Red is not compulsory. In fact, any colour will do. Using a felt tipped marker, however, feels more satisfying than pressing down with a hard thin pencil.

Curious combinations of desired books lined up on my cart as I proceeded from shelf to shelf: *The Mennonite Solid Food Cookbook*, *Semiotics for Dummies*, *The Official Guide For Identifying UFOS*, *Grease Girl: Advanced Auto Mechanics* and *How to Find and Keep Your Perfect Mate*—a slender, well-thumbed volume, written in point form.

I labelled each item and dropped it in the appropriate grey plastic shipping box behind the circulation desk.

Brian Bartlett
FOOT-DOCTOR FOR THE HOMELESS

Day after day, I see more toenails than eyes.
I'd push the truth if I said my office
is smaller than my patients' cardboard shelters,
but it's more cramped than most. The floor tiles curl
at the edges, the light bulbs are bare, and Hank
might hear Horace's cracking joints behind the screen.
Only a few old men called me "Ma'am," like I was
a teacher from their childhoods more distant
than death.
          Years ago when the devils of arthritis started
needling my feet, I withdrew from General Practice,
learned everything I could about ankles, heels, shins,
the metatarsal and the phalanges, the way a rabbi
dissects Deuteronomy. I've unknotted laces
that fell apart like spaghetti, peeled off
running shoes that erupted like abscesses.

More than shirts or hats, shoes tell stories—
of chafings and stumbles, a thousand weathers,
a schizophrenic's circular miles trod,
trod, trod. Famous footwear—Cinderella's,

Chaplin's—are odourless in the face of the real.
I've seen no feet I would dry with my hair.
They're the colour of mushrooms, wilted roses,
eggplant skin. Hands rubber-gloved, I swear
feet have voices, words arising from blisters
and broken flesh, not from mouths and beards.
Those voices tell me, mumbling or unexpectedly
clear, rasping or childlike, of frostbitten nights in parks,
skinhead stormtrooper boots, a door forced shut
where the clean and moneyed are wanted.

When the feet twitch with monologues, I can't get a word
in edgewise against the jagged curses and
laughter, all entangled with enemies and wraiths.
Then I feel like some doctor in hell, a fire
burning at my door. The poor and the miserable
were cast there not for punishment, but merely
by the whims of whatever does the casting.
Some nights at home, I stare at my feet
projecting beyond the tub's foam: afflicted
but lucky. Back on the street, the homeless might hobble
less, but trailing my fingers in lavender oil I ask
who will bandage their minds, who will pour ointment
onto their nerves? When I write out slips
for the pharmacy or the hospital, I'm never sure if

they'll reach other hands, or flutter down the sidewalk
in a wet wind. As I pull the plug of my bath,
I've pictured my prescriptions and referrals,
like prayers ending mid-sentence, sluiced away
                              in the street's rain.

THE SONOGRAPHER

—for Al Moritz

Call me Broadcaster of the Early Heartbeat,
First Examiner of the Head's Circumference,
He Who Sees Your Child First. Call me
young Mr. Faith, Mr. Hope. I could say
"high-frequency sound waves going at
five-to-seven-million miles per second."
A fine science, this. Most days it's business
as usual; but when the commonness of it all
subsides, for a few seconds it seems—dare I say—
sacramental, and I recall holding my wife's hand,
watching our son turning like a shadowy fish
on the screen (not "ghostly form,"
ghostliness being on the other side of life).

I'm the coroner's sunny double, his lucky brother.
Just once, I'd have us switch places
to spare him dark questions and bloody probings
for a night. I wonder if he'd bow
to the consummate promise of a fetus forming—

if he'd weep to be in my shoes.
On vacation, I get hungry for the moment
when a shoulder or foot comes into view,
the opposite of dissolving. It gets addictive, this gentle
saying to strangers, "There it is—see?"
Once I sat all week on a Cuban beach with the sky
like an empty screen, and I would've been glad
to see a cloud as small as a kneecap.

The news, of course, isn't always cheering. Then
what I see straightens my mouth, tightens a knot
in my throat. I've jotted symbols you don't want
to grasp, but Drs. MacKeigan or Varma or Finch
deliver the news. I see, and say nothing, guilty
I'm spared the job. I've seen celebration drain
from eyes in an instant, then a week later
struggle back, stubborn, giving a welcome at last.
"Sweet one," they whisper, ". . .angel."

Who can see hope more clearly than I, day
after day?—a shadowy hand turning this way,
a thumb going to a mouth, like a joke

at our gazing, our impatience. I'm one of fate's
surveyors. Maybe it's a right no one
should have—to be an eavesdropper on the future,
always the first on board to spot
a thin beautiful line of land barely lifting
                      above the horizon and the sea.

Marilyn Bowering
WHY ARE YOU HERE, MY DEAR STUDENTS?

Why are you here, my dear students?
You should be filling your lungs with literature
Your souls with the love of the world
Why aren't you on my doorstep, so full of longing
For poetry that you'll suffer in the cold
Until I let you in and reveal my secrets?

Have I told you my story?
All night I wrote in a kitchen overrun
With mice to have a poem worthy of my teacher
The small black mice had a hay-day with the garbage
They broke the rubber seal of the refrigerator
And skated along the shelves: what mouldered cheeses they found
What aged vegetables!

What a trial it was to remain with my back to them
And hear their scrabble, the testing twitter of a hundred
Mouse beats, and write my semblance of poetry. What else
Did I have to bring to my master?
What have *you* given me, I ask you
But your faith that I can solve the world's enmity
To poets; that within the grading system there's a key

I keep just out of reach
The golden door, my dear ones, is near
Don't listen to a word I say; sleep on the doorstep
Of a poet: there's a certain coming and going
The passage of all the other poets who visit
You must suffer the depredations of vermin
    until you can hear them
Oh, they'll say, Here's a new one, what will we do
    with him or her?
Lift them up, and bring them in for soup?

When you revive and your lungs are sufficiently warmed
    and full of literature
And when the fragments of your hearts reveal themselves
    as letters
Kept safely just for you, then hold a pen and begin your addresses
Oh my dear ones, my beloved
Students who I fail constantly to inspire in the classroom
    —only then
Will you know what it is I have to teach you

April Bulmer
OFFICE SUPPLIES

I am a woman of the clock.
My watch beats
like my heart:
cogs and a jewel.

All day shadows move.
My hand like a crow.
It dreams of a sturdy bough.

My desk is oak.
Drawer open like a mouth.
It speaks of paperclips and glue.

I rise at night with poetry.
Books of bark and caribou.
Words like hieroglyphs.
They fly as birds
from the nest on my tongue

All day I balance paper.
Imagine gusts of wind.
Invoices lifting like prayers
above my stained coffee cup.

Barry Callaghan
MELLOW YELLOW

The McBrides lived in a comfortable house in a row of red brick houses on the south side of Amelia Street. There were tall sheltering elms and a stone wall on the north side of the street, a wall that enclosed the old cemetery, and beyond the cemetery was a railroad track, a single line that was used only early in the morning when Marie-Claire would waken to a low train whistle and get up and look out over the stones, many of the thin slabs tilted and broken. She'd played in the cemetery as a child. She had stretched out on her stomach and called down into the earth and listened, and called again, and listened. No one had answered. She'd decided that no one was there, that she was safe inside the walls, so the first time she'd let a boy touch her naked body had been in the long tufted grass, lying between the stones, but he'd been so frightened of the dead and her white body in the failing light of dusk that he'd suddenly stood up and run away to the door in the wall.

At nineteen, her full breasts trembled when she walked quickly. She had long legs and auburn hair down to her shoulders. Boys whistled at her when she walked down the street. She didn't mind. Sometimes she put two fingers to her mouth, as her father had taught her, and whistled back. She didn't like young men her own age. She liked men who were old enough to be serious, but that didn't mean she liked old men. Older men weren't serious, she said, they were worried about dying. She never thought about death, even when she went for a walk in the graveyard. She felt wonderfully alone and at ease with herself among the stones, alive and eager to see the world. That's why she thought the morning train whistle was like a call and on some mornings as the train rumbled slowly past the yard, she leaned against her window pane and let out a low muffled wail, calling to the train, giddy with expectation as she went down to breakfast where her mother said to her, "Whatever in the world are you going to do with your life?" and she said, "I don't know, but I'm going to live it."

She brought Conrad Zingg to the house to have supper with her mother and father. She had been seeing him for several months and her mother had said that she wanted to meet him. "This is Conrad," she said, and her mother smiled because he was tall and slender with a lot of black hair, a firm mouth, and a steady dark eye. "Call me Connie," he said, taking her father's hand but smiling at her mother. He seemed very sure of himself, very amiable, and yet aloof. "Yes, all my friends call me Connie," he said and stepped back, shoving his hands into his suitcoat pockets. Her father stepped back, too, disconcerted. "Connie, eh," he said. "Connie what?"

"Connie Zingg."

"Zingg, what kind of a name is Zingg?"

"Viennese. My parents came from Vienna when I was a child."

"So you grew up here, then?"

"This is my town," he said.

"And here you are," Mrs. McBride said, "at home in our house for supper," and she said to her husband, "And doesn't Marie-Claire look happy." Conrad said, "Zingg went the strings of her heart." Mrs. McBride laughed and took him by the arm and led him into the small dining room. Marie-Claire was startled. She felt a tinge of betrayal. She didn't think they should be talking about her heart, taking for granted how she felt, even though she had wakened that morning wondering as she listened to the train, if she didn't love him.

She tried to think of how she would tell him after supper that he shouldn't joke about her feelings, but then as they stood by the table her thoughts drifted back to the afternoon they had spent together on the bay. They had laughed and laughed, riding the ferry, not getting off, but pretending that they were docking at all the great cities, and as she had stared at the sunlight on the choppy waves, she'd felt that she was wonderfully safe beside him, safe in the shelter of his self-possession, safe to dream that she could be anywhere she wanted to be in the world. "Well, sit down," her father said. "Marie-Claire, she says you work at being a traffic consultant. What's that?"

"I design the traffic downtown."

"You dress it up?" her mother said.

"No, no," he said affably. "Computers, I work out the timing, the red and green lights, trying to get the flow."

"Stop and go," her father said.

"Right."

"You're in charge of the stop and go?"

"Right."

They ate their supper. It was a good supper of pot roast and potatoes. Marie-Claire was pleased because her mother was happy. She knew her mother was lonely for company. She also knew that her father was morosely uncomfortable, eating with a stranger in his home. He thought a home was a safe place for friends where he didn't have to explain himself. He did not have many friends. But Conrad had been very attentive to her father's silences. He had not talked too much or been overbearing. At the end of the evening, after saying goodnight to her parents, he kissed her lightly at the front door and said, "Salt of the earth, your people, salt of the earth."

Her father was still at the table as she passed to go upstairs, content that she'd shown her parents that a successful young man could be attracted to her and could want to court her, but her father called out, "It doesn't work."

"What?" she asked startled.

"The stop and go. Any damn fool can see that."

"Nonsense," she said angrily.

"He may have designed it, but it doesn't work."

She got into bed feeling wounded, as if her father had passed judgement not only on Conrad but on her, and for a moment she wanted to rush downstairs and say as cruelly as she could, "What do you know, what have you ever designed?" but she was naked in her bed and too tired to get dressed again. "Tomorrow is another day," she said and went to sleep.

She admired Conrad's confidence, and how sure he said he was that he had a future. Her mother and father had always talked about the future as a day to be afraid of, a day when everything would go wrong. As she listened to Conrad talk she tried to keep a grave expression on her face. She wanted him to take her seriously. He talked about traffic, and how his control of where and when people went was crucial to the control of chaos. "Red and green, in themselves they don't mean anything," he said. "It's like right and wrong. Red and green. Life's that simple, and that hard."

"I like yellow," she said, though she'd never thought about it before, and in fact, with her auburn hair, she did not think she looked good in yellow.

He laughed. "You're priceless," he said.

"So are you," she said, sitting cross-legged on a sofa in his apartment, watching him throw darts at a yellow and black board he had put up on the door to the hall. Sometimes, he would play by himself for an hour, touching each steel tip of a dart to his tongue, quietly counting down numbers as the darts hit the board. "You've got to not only learn how to count down," he said, "you've got to think backwards." She did not understand why he wanted to think backwards or how he could watch darts programs on the sports television network, sometimes for two hours, hardly talking to her. He would glance at her, as if he were going to speak, but all too often he had the back of his hand against his mouth. He liked to sit with his hand like that, and once she had said, "Are you chewing your knuckle?"

"No, of course not," he'd said and he'd put his hand defensively down on his knee, but she had seen that his knuckle was red, almost raw.

"Do I frighten you?" she'd asked impetuously.

"Don't be silly," he'd said. "A slip of a girl like you?"

"Do you want to arm wrestle?" she'd said.

"I'd break your wrist," he'd said, rubbing his inflamed knuckle. "Yes, I would."

"No you wouldn't," she'd said.

One evening, he asked to meet her a little earlier than usual so that they could take a walk before going out to supper. She wore a simple black raw silk dress. His hair was cut. He was very erect as they passed several expensive stores. He gave her an approving smile and folded her arm under his. Then he stopped by a jewelry store window and asked which ring she liked, and when she said she wasn't looking for a ring, he grew sullen and distant.

"I don't like diamonds," she said. "I like pearls."

"Diamonds are a girl's best friend," he said.

"Not this girl. And I don't like red roses either," she said, trying to take a light impish air. "Yellow, white, anything but red." He said nothing. For some inexplicable reason as they walked along the street in silence she felt guilty, as if she had failed him.

She asked him where they were going.

"Why, we're going to The Senator."

The Senator was an expensive supper club, a sophisticated jazz lounge. He led her up the stairs and through the door, and she let him hold her hand as if he were guiding her, certain that there was a grace in her stride because she had studied how all the models in the fashion films on television walked. She could see that he was pleased with her, because he walked beside her with his shoulders squared, an almost stern and disdainful look in his eyes that might have frightened her if she hadn't been so sure he was like this only because he wanted to have her.

The head waiter pointed to a side table, but Conrad took the waiter's arm firmly and nodded to the front. "We'll sit down by Mr. Jackson...thanks...he'll be glad to see us..."

"But sir..."

"No buts about it."

"Sir..."

"Thank you..."

Conrad, with a quick wave of his arm, almost

as if he were directing traffic—which made her laugh gaily—led her through the close tables and then when they were seated he leaned across to her before they ordered drinks, and said, "Today is my birthday."

"Your birthday...Why didn't you tell me...I should be taking you out...I don't have anything for you."

"You're all I want," he said, looking directly at her.

She put her head in her hands for a moment and let out a low quiet wailing sound. He looked perplexed, "What was that?" he asked.

"That's how I whistle in the dark," she said, trying to laugh.

He looked very grave and she thought he was watching her as if he were trying to trace her thoughts. She sat back in her chair. The week before, he had told her that she had to make up her mind about their future, and he had given her until his birthday to decide, but she was sure he hadn't told her when his birthday was, and she hadn't given it any thought at all. Only now, with the steadiness in his eyes, did she realize that he had been serious.

She pouted. It was ridiculous to suddenly thrust such a decision on her. How could she decide? Though they had been close, they had had wonderful moments in which she'd felt both safe and free, and though they'd made love several times, he had never really talked about love. He had never said that he loved her though he had said one night that he valued her more than anything he had in the world. She had wanted to cry when he'd said that, but now she thought, he's never said that he actually loves me and she resented his restraint and his self-assurance. "Well," she thought, "when he mentions it we can talk it out."

J.J. Jackson, the pianist, came to their table. He greeted Conrad warmly, calling him Connie, and then said, "You got yourself a fine-looking lady. *Fine*." Conrad asked him to sit down, and before she could tartly say that she thought she had a *fine*-looking man, Jackson told her that he had met Conrad in the Night Traffic Court. He said he'd been charged with "something really stupid, entering into a left turn lane when the light was already yellow, stopping and then turning against the red." Conrad, he said, had suddenly offered to appear as a witness for him. "He was some kinda brilliant," Jackson said. "He had that judge all turned around inside his head, with the time of this and the time of that, and how this and that were impossible, and finally, this here judge, he says, 'How do you know all this?' and he says, 'Because I designed the whole system, your honour,' and I thought I'd laugh till I died at the look on that judge's face." Jackson smacked him hard on the back. "My main man," he said. "My ace boon coon." Conrad accepted this display of warmth with ease. He looked so satisfied that she wondered if he hadn't seen Jackson's wry, belittling smirk and wondered why he would let anyone smack him so hard on the back. When Jackson left, Conrad settled into his reserved aloof air, the back of his hand against his mouth. She reached out and touched his free hand that was flat on the table and he smiled again, looking directly at her, a silent resolve in his eyes.

She shrugged and said, "What's it like being a boon coon?" and then, indignantly, she enjoyed the music, clapping enthusiastically after one of Jackson's solos, and the crowd around her was clapping loudly, too, so she put two fingers in her mouth, and she whistled. She was frightened that she might be acting like a young girl but it was the only way she felt she could maintain her sense of herself, her sense of her own dignity. So she whistled again and wanted to cry. She couldn't understand why she wanted to cry and why he refused to say anything to her about their relationship.

They left the lounge and walked home, taking the side streets that were quiet in the night. It had turned cool and she was shivering, yet she didn't cuddle against him as they walked. She didn't feel she could because he was walking with his hands in his suitjacket pockets. He talked about baseball and a woman who was trying to swim across Lake Ontario for charity, for crippled children, and he seemed not only concerned about the children but quite content with her, but she knew he was not content and she thought he was not being honest, not being fair. She was angry and refused to walk all the way home in resigned silence.

"Would you like this to be our last night, Connie?"

"That's up to you..."

"No it's not," she said fiercely and wheeled away, furious, but somehow she knew that if she said any more he would just smile at her. She knew she would never forgive him if he smiled at her in her rage. She remembered how he had smiled at her in The Senator, as if he were being patient with her. She was tempted to put two fingers in her mouth and whistle at him. Instead, she punched him on the arm. "You're something else," she said.

"And so are you," he said.

They stood at the bottom of the stairs to her veranda. He was suddenly talking to her again, as if they had not been silent almost all the way home, and he was talking about how he hoped to move out of traffic control into policy planning for the whole city. "But never into politics," he said. "You just get your brains beaten in in politics and beaten in by any clunkhead who comes along." He told her it took courage to plan for the future, to go to the top. "That's the way it is at city hall," he said, "the politicians, the dorks who don't know what they're doing, they are on the ground floor, the planners are on the top floor." He kissed her lightly on the cheek. Then, after a moment in which he held her hand, looking down as if he were meditative and shy, he said, "Goodnight Marie-Claire..."

He began to turn away.

"Connie...just a minute, Connie..."

There were tears in her eyes.

"Connie, don't go away yet..."

He turned to her eagerly, expectantly, and she felt very young, very unknowing, beside him. He seemed to have counted on her calling out.

"Connie..."

He touched her cheek, as if his touch could help her out of her confusion, but she didn't feel confused. She felt bullied by his silence. She wanted to slap his face and tell him he was pig-headed and arrogant. "I guess I'm just yellow," she said.

"What?"

"Yellow."

"There's no need to be scared," he said.

"Who said I'm scared? You don't know what I'm talking about, do you? You don't know where the hell I'm coming from."

She turned and walked calmly up the stairs and into the house, leaving him standing on the walk. For a moment, as she peeked through the lace curtains covering the small oval glass window in the door, she thought he was going to come up the stairs and her heart leapt, but then he turned and walked across the street and stood against the cemetery wall. At first, she thought she could feel him willing her out of the house, to come to him and she was afraid, but then, as she watched him stand for so long in the shadows with his back to the wall and his hand to his mouth, she thought he looked lonely and lost and she was sure he was waiting for her, as he had waited all night, because he couldn't bring himself to cross the street, couldn't say that he wanted her, couldn't say that he loved her. She felt a sudden urge to comfort him, to go to him and hold him and say "You want to arm wrestle, never mind, you win," but then she thought with contempt, *He'd be scared stiff if I ever took him off into the graveyard at night*. She turned away from the door, turned off the hall light and went into the kitchen where her mother and father were having their bedtime cup of tea.

As she saw them sitting so quietly at the table, as they had sat for years, she felt young and even more confident about her life, and yet she also felt ashamed that she had not been more of a friend to her mother and father in their home. She kissed her startled mother on the forehead and then, full of a strange new mellowness, she draped her arms around her father's neck and said "You're right, it doesn't work."

"What?" he asked, astonished.

"The stop and go, it doesn't work."

She went upstairs to bed. She couldn't wait to go to sleep and then wake in the morning to the call of the train whistle coming to her across the graveyard.

James Clarke
BUSINESS MEETING

The boss orders an early morning conference
in the airless boardroom.
        Attendance mandatory.
Smiles stuck on too tight stray in
with his morning coffee.
His words: "You may sit in any chair, but
don't sit in mine."
The auditor's report is two hundred pages long.
What was he thinking?
For the third consecutive quarter results disappoint.
        "Top Dog" is not amused.
Who'll be whacked this time, I muse.
The minutes drag on,
our laptops signal sleep.
For a while the meeting dangles
        between crisis & resolution,
then yawns into grayout.
After the fourth coffee I ask myself:
Who can I strangle?

Back at my desk I drift through the afternoon
shuffling papers,
        pretending to care.
Just as I'm about to leave to catch the early Go-Train
a pink slip, unseen yet half foreseen
floats down out of nowhere.

ENTREPRENEURIAL DISCRETION

After the lawyer asked the bespectacled
businessman in the blue suit
what he did for a living, silence fell
over the courtroom. The lawyer repeated
the question.
"I'd rather not say," the witness answered.

That's when I stepped in to remind him
that this was a court of law, that witnesses
are obliged to answer all questions.
"To tell you the truth, your Honour," he said,
looking me in the eye, "I'm
putting the finishing touches on my
invention to liquidate the national debt
in two years."
"The national debt in two years?" I said.
"How do you expect to do that?"

The witness smiled at me
as though I were a child. "Now
Your Honour, I wouldn't be much of a
businessman if I tipped my hand, would I?"
"I guess not," I replied. "Mum's the word."

Brian Campbell
PANTOUM OF A HIRED MAN

He woke to dawn's grey tombstone light.
Faces he met that day were a blur.
Each day seemed like any other:
A fidging of channels, all the same.

Faces he met that day were a blur:
If they said hello, he said hello back.
Fidging of channels it was, all the same.
Riding on subways, he felt like a number.

If they said hello, he said hello back:
If they asked him how he was, he said, "I feel fine."
But riding on subways, he felt like a number.
If he showed up or didn't, it didn't really matter.

If they asked him how he was, he said, "I feel fine."
And the wife was good, the kids were great,
But if he showed up or didn't, it didn't really matter:
Within him, a strife he could not define.

And the wife was good, the kids were great.
When he wandered into rooms, he wondered why,

Within him a strife he could not define.
All was decided: no need to complain.

When he wandered into rooms, he wondered why.
She was there, they were there; pleasure, and laughter.
All was decided: no need to complain.
He had his papers and tasks, so what was he after?

She was there, they were there, and pleasure, and laughter,
But words like "drag" and "heartache" came quickly to mind.
He had his papers and tasks, so what was he after?
This too would prove hard —oh, so hard—to define.

Words like "drag" and "heartache" came quickly to mind.
Each day seemed like every single other.
Faces he met were always a blur
As dawn dimmed to dusk: grey tombstone light.

Sue Chenette
WHY I LIKE MY CAR HEATER

Do not think poorly of me if I tell you
that after teaching piano lessons all day,
one child following another, the weight
of their progress or lack thereof carried
from one half hour to the next, my smile
a little boat filled with coaxing
a curved finger, graceful phrase, it is

bliss to walk to my car—especially
in winter, in chill dusk—
to unlock the door, sling in
my bag, turn the ignition and
the heater knob, then swing out
from my parking spot and bask, cozied
in solitude through the darkening streets.

Brandon Crilly
THE BLACK ROOM

Even before graduating from teacher's college, David had heard rumours of the "black room." It was supposed to be the place teachers were sent while they were under investigation. He knew it wasn't real, just the teacher's version of the boogeyman. That didn't stop him from imagining what it might be like.

When he pictured it, he saw himself in a classroom. There was sunlight shining through the windows, reflecting off the empty chalkboard and the usual motivational posters. The old clock above the door read quarter-to-twelve, nearly time for lunch. The classroom almost seemed normal. Instead of students seated in the desks, though, it was teachers, each absorbed in their own thoughts while they waited for the day to end.

He imagined it the same way each time. David was sitting at the back. He stared at the unopened book on his desk and wondered if he was one of the slackers now, if he had devolved from the overachiever he used to be. No matter how much he willed it, he couldn't bring himself to open the book. Its title, *Exercises in Professional Conduct*, glared up at him in disappointment.

There were others with him, fellow teachers he had heard about through internal emails or the evening news. Seated two desks in front of him was Natalie Kerrick, who looked like she stepped out of a Victorian novel with her blouse buttoned up to the neck, skirt almost to her ankles, and hair tied in a tight bun. David suspected she dressed that way in order to help her case, as the board investigated her for overt sexuality in her English classes. The way Natalie hunched over her desk, occasionally shuddering with sobs like she had during her only news interview, made David think she was wrongly accused. Unless Drama was her other teaching subject.

Two desks to her right, Vic Bailey was cracking his knuckles. The board's rumour mill said he used those knuckles on his school's quarterback during practice, when the quarterback challenged him for working the team too hard. Even at fifty-five, Vic was huge and menacing; he looked like the kind of guy who might have been a bouncer before becoming certified to teach. David sometimes wondered how one of those knuckles would feel against his face. As tough as he looked, Vic had said over and over that he was sorry for snapping, and that he wanted nothing more than to keep coaching football.

The oddest one was Lindsay Sappoli, a thirty-something Math teacher seated near the front. She was another one that made the news, likely because people couldn't figure out if she'd had a nervous breakdown, had been overcome with desperation, or if she was simply nuts. Everyone knew Lindsay's story: how she gave a student the keys to her Camaro to pick her up a pregnancy test, terrified after the night before, and how that student crashed the Camaro and broke his arm after running a stop sign. The others at least had hope, but David figured Lindsay was done as a teacher. He wondered if the board would recommend locking her up as well as firing her.

There was only one teacher in that imagined room who didn't seem the least bit sorry for his actions or worried about his career. Riley Jones was leaning back in his chair with his feet propped up on his desk, arms behind his head, smiling with his eyes closed. He had only been a teacher for three years, and David wondered how many young girls he had seduced in that time. He figured there had to be more than just the one who'd gone to the police. The smug smile and the casual shrugs that came with every shot of Riley on the news made him Public Enemy Number One for other teachers, the worst example of the profession but the only one a lot of people saw. Riley would start whistling a tune every time David imagined him, until Vic made a low growling sound and Riley stopped, his smile growing wider.

Everything about that black room—the other teachers, the near-silence, the unopened conduct book—made him feel worse. David looked up at the others again and wondered for the hundredth time, *I'm not like them, am I? Do I really belong here?*

When the fire alarm went off at his high school, David had assumed like everyone else that it was just a drill. Since he didn't have a class that period, his job was to check the boys' washrooms on the second floor. He found them empty, and soon joined everyone outside, calmly waiting for the all-clear signal from the principal. It took a few minutes for them to notice the smoke coming from the back of the school and realize the fire was real. By the time the fire department arrived, the flames were spreading. The teachers and students were ushered further away. Three-quarters of the school were destroyed, including half of the second floor.

The next day, David learned about the body in the second floor boys' washroom, the one in the north corner. The coroner identified it as Ben Kwong, a ninth-grade student. It didn't take long for the police to call David, asking if he had checked the upstairs bathrooms like he was supposed to. David assured them he did. He thought they believed him, until his principal told him to stay home while they determined if he was at fault.

He sat at home waiting for the board's judgment, spending hours imagining that black room and the teachers who were sent there. It was easier to picture that place than to keeping playing out his actions in his head, trying to remember if he checked every stall, if he called out to see if anyone was there and flicked the lights in case a student was deaf or using an iPod. The more he thought about it, the more the voice in the back of his head convinced him he'd forgotten to do something, or been too lazy, and that Ben Kwong was dead because of it.

So he imagined the black room instead, and compared himself to the others.

I'm not like them, am I? These people all made mistakes, that's why they're here. Did I make a mistake, too?

In his mind, Riley was whistling again, and Natalie had started sobbing. David looked down at the book on his desk, wishing it would answer his questions, give him some kind of reassurance that everything would be fine.

The book didn't comply. He knew it could only help him if he actually opened it. He was tempted to smile; he would have given the same suggestion to one of his students if they were waiting for answers from an unopened book. *Because I'm a good teacher, right?*

The book didn't answer that question either.

Cyril Dabydeen
CONVERSATION

I live in a bureaucratic town—
there's so much paper work here
& people, longing for power
(so you say)
no, I'm not cynical—
dear God, help me to be close to real people
& to the things that affect my senses—
let me also continue to renew myself
this day, night—
it is my eternal
        desire.

Carlinda D'Alimonte
FISSURES

In the stillness of the room
fifty-eight eyes
twenty-nine quiet mouths
attentive, wondering.

I skim faces, have learned to soften my focus.
There is too much
we will need to know
later.

Later, a series of minor quakes and after shocks
when I return yesterday's work—you on leaflets of paper
where I have said,
Yes, you have done this. No, develop this further.
Consider the order here. Watch those prepositions.
A preposition is a word that...
And the final abomination—
a number: 65, 79, 84.

Later it is your turn:
Some converge on me.

But I am a nineties student.
You don't understand. You don't like me.
She got higher than me? That's not fair.
This is my opinion. My opinion can't be wrong.
Miss, can I talk to you?
I can do better than this.
In the background, a cacophony of voices:
I'm happy. I really worked hard.
I deserve more. She likes the girls better. What a joke!
I didn't even finish the book.
This is so subjective; if she doesn't like you you're screwed.

My attention shifts and I wonder
what questions will not be asked
by those who silently sit at their desks
perusing pages.

Gathering the notes of my lesson,
I respond to my inquisitors,
We will have to talk about his
later.
I walk to front and centre:
Let's move on for now to Waiting for Godot.

But there are fissures in the room,
some gaping cracks, some tiny lines almost imperceptible,
and we are aware of being somewhere new,
all of us gripping more firmly
the floor
or the edges of our desks,
or the fine pages that lie between our fingers.

Christopher Doda
A SAD EFFECT OF TENURE

Late last year, as fading winter light
Struck the window of his spacious office,
Professor Don Cohen pondered flesh

And God in history: "Old gods were men
Writ large, reactions to fate and weather,
Storms and seasons, love and lust and fresh

Needs to beg the universe to behave
Against its natural inclination. Because
The body of man (my own) is 80% water,

Elder gods understood that it owned
Men, their wells, their ships, their lives.
Yet our God, (my own) has no flesh,"

Thought Dr. Cohen, "and thus no water.
But I am created in His image. Therefore
I see a great statistical possibility

That my flesh has none of God, as I
Can be no more than 20% of He who
Creates but does not participate, has

Made a world 70% covered in water
That He is not part of; therefore what
Separates God and matter is water.

(How odd I thought He was made of fire.)
Therefore God is a theory. Therefore God
Is a familiar motive. Therefore God is a painful

Manoeuvre. Therefore God lives in a language
Of one: an inviolable universe. Therefore God
Is a mechanism. Therefore He is greased

With oil, a series of movable parts,
And therefore He breaks down but does
Not decompose. Therefore I drink

With a purpose. Therefore I am a fish."

Paula Eisenstein
SHIPS AT SEA

I'm the fifth cubicle from the window of my aisle at the government call centre where I work. Someone I trained with came by my desk and observed I pin up a lot of yellow sticky notes on my baffle. A baffle is the soft fabric covering the partitions separating the different cubicles you can pin things on. That's what she noticed about my desk space. It's funny when people notice things about you, you didn't realize.

Some of the sticky notes actually say the same things because one of the computer programs we run is enormous and archaic and I hardly ever use it unless I have to, so sometimes I accidently put up a sticky note reminding me how to do something I don't do that often that I already put up before. I have a helpful attitude towards myself. Even if I don't always take myself up on it.

My colleagues and I run many programs simultaneously. There's a lot of information we need to be able to access. I actually feel fairly magnificent controlling all those applications at the same time, like a captain of a large sailing ship at sea. Even if the person in the cubicle right beside me on the other side of the separating partition between us is sailing her own magnificent galleon too. And even if we really were sailing ships they would collide and make a big mess and everyone would drown in the high rolling waves.

Before I got the person who's sitting beside me now I had a really mean person. She was really ugly too. When I ate food at my desk she didn't like the smell of she would go and report it to my supervisor and not even say anything to me first. Then my supervisor would call me to his desk and say, I understand you like spicy food. And I would say, if you call a salad I bought at Cultures spicy. But he hadn't heard of Cultures so for all he knew Cultures' food was spicy.

Then she could hear me chewing gum through the partition and told me to stop but when I forgot and was chewing too loudly again that her foster-mother said chewing gum is disgusting and not for ladies.

But telling me it was her foster-mother completely gave away probably why she was so mean; she hadn't had a proper mother-bond when she was growing up. Then at Christmas she gave me a Christmas card that included her husband's, her dog's and her fish's name. Making conversation about it despite my bad feelings toward her got her laughing about the adorable interestingness of herself and her fish name signing to the lady in the cubicle on the other side of her cubicle who she'd known for a long time and who was nice to her maybe because she was used to her, yet remained nice to me at the same time. The mood was festive.

Then she was leaving. I was glad but didn't gloat when I stood up to go to the bathroom or on break and was looking over our partition directly down into her desk area. She had decided to leave for a short term placement in another office for a change. Not that she told me personally; an email distributed to the team from our supervisor advised me of the change. Usually I don't complain about people. Really. But with her I told my friends over lunch in the lunch room how mean she was and they looked at her and in a glance all agreed they could see it too.

The new person who moved in to her cubicle asked if I would please try seeing how I liked having the overhead fluorescent office light turned out because you can ask for that in our office if the people around you agree to it. I said I was willing to give it a try. What a difference turning off that light made. I instantly felt such a relief. So of course I said, no problem, let's leave the light out. Perhaps it made the new person like me more but that's not why I did it.

I have no regrets even if it is darker. Even if it is harder to read the little yellow sticky notes on the baffle than it used to be. What I could do is make a request for a seat at the beginning of one of the cubicle aisles beside the window. Then the light wouldn't be stressful fluorescent light. It would be natural sunlight. But I wouldn't want to ask to move because I wouldn't know who I'd be sitting beside if they moved me. I might get someone awful again.

Since ours is the phone line for pensioners we get a lot of calls from elderly people. Last Thursday, after I helped an old lady sort out a problem she was having, she said, bless your heart. It's not the first time. My posture straightens and my heart feels all light and aglow when it gets blessed.

Jesse Patrick Ferguson
PUSH PINS AGAINST FORGETTING

Bell rings and they go and the voice draws their pencil
like a sled across snow; when its runners are frozen
rope snaps and the voice then is pulling no burden
but runs like a dog on the winter of paper.
—P.K. Page, "The Stenographers"

His human-resource abilities would bring a tear to your eye.
He keeps few sharp things in his desk drawers. Push-pins
against forgetting. Pin Man. Pens in a tasteful mug:
   Individuality,
little "I." In spare moments, he raps fingers on the sill
of his hard-won window, double-paned, and counts the taps,
then attempts to beat his record. He records all, or tries.
For fifty-six minutes, he watches office girls eat until
bell rings and they go and the voice draws their pencil,

laptop, blackberry, etc., to some other floor
where he has little reason to follow. In the interest
of avoiding a pinch (before he forgets) he begins
next year's schedule. Takes the receiver tightly in hand
as though he could squeeze blood from a phone,

and he gives blood, too, during the company drive. Last year,
in fact, he prodded his team to give pints by the dozen.
Like a sled across snow, when its runners are frozen

and the mountain is high, report after report slides,
as though of its own will, onto his desk. He has a date
with each and touches the tip of his red pen
to the soft of his tongue, like a lover, before he begins.
Someone waits for him at home, and he longs for her
to learn HTML, XML or shorthand. He'd send his love,
but his Internet usage is being monitored. A quick call, then:
rope snaps and the voice then is pulling no burden.

Working late, love. Love, this quarter got away from us.
Might be the death of us. I keep forgetting Item 1.
Item 2: remember Item 1. Also, clear desk.
Cluttered desk begets mind of clutter—a thought he considers
worthy of the corporate handbook, corporate posterity.
An original thought, perhaps. Should jot it before it slips away.
He scribbles on a daffodil Post-It; it clings no better
but runs like a dog on the winter of paper.

WHAT'S HIS FACE

An infinitely forgettable fellow,
What's His Face came and went
in a funk of obscurity. He often had half a mind
to this or that, but dissipated such
thoughts through half-hearted measures.
Wives in the checkout line gossiped
while thumbing through *People*
and dropped his name with no intention
to pick it up again.
                "What's His Face,"
they remarked, "at a dinner party
is usually good for a cut-rate
bottle of Sauvignon, something with cheese.
Perhaps he'll venture an anecdote
colourless as a cocktail onion
that slips through your fingers
and winds up forgotten, petrified
beneath the chesterfield."

His departure was rarely marked;
at some point he'd be simply gone,
his empties, likewise.

               He was middle
management at who-knows-where, where they do
something to or with computers.
It was there he met his one true love
who one night, whilst they two
were engaged in you-know-what,
suddenly saw what all her girlfriends
had failed to see in What's His Face.
The following day, she and his co-workers
could be seen laughing him out of face
by the water cooler.

And so between office and exit
he may still stride the linoleum mile,
his necktie a mocking
interrogation mark. He may reflect on
the frosted glass of door and room divider:
What's His Face beneath fluorescent tubes,
complexion grey as linoleum tile.

Marty Gervais
THE WHITE SHIRT

We wore white shirts
We'd fan out in the morning light
racing up Bay Street
to the Toronto Stock Exchange
barely 18
hair slicked back
gleaming black brogues
dark blazer
purple tie
our world of 1965 defined
in black and white
like the newspaper
the Leafs and Canadiens
our television sets
our politics
chess board pieces
And the white shirt
was our ticket
It carried us into the
commerce of this new world
when we rose each morning

in autumnal darkness
steam pressing it like
a wrinkled map
with an iron
borrowed from the boarding house
making sure of the edges
running the iron
in between the buttons
and over the pocket
and careful for
the sleeves on both sides
and never forgetting
the back side
and the shirt felt warm
on the shoulder blades
only for an instant
when I pulled it on
We were young men
of a new age
and we sailed
those mornings up
Bay Street
eager to fill out pockets
confident that it would be the shirt
that would do all the talking

Steven Heighton
NOUGHTS & CROSSES

An unsent reply

—―――-**Original Message**——-
From: <j.in.corydon@hotmail.com>
To: <nella_biagini@sympatico.ca>
Sent: April 22, 2007 1:16 AM
Subject: RE: Hello?

n,
yes yes i did get your email but needed to reflect a little. i'm
sorry. and i do think it might be best if i pulled back a little now,
i seem to need some space to hear my own breathing, my own
thoughts, it is hard when we are always in dialogue. i am sorry
if this feels abrupt or my reasons feel vague, they just must be.
for one thing, as i guess i implied, i have been asked to keep secrets
and want to keep my word. i know you understand. you, after
all are one of my secrets. and as you know yourself and even said,
maybe a severing, a temporary severing is what's best now,
for both of you. for everyone involved. please don't worry about
me, i will be all right, i am determined to get through this time. i
promise i will get in touch again when i feel i can.

love always,
j

* * *

n

As in: never again, never again. That phrase with its cardiac cadence. Slight arrhythmia. A certain tunnelled clump of muscle misbehaving, missing steps or taking clumsy extras, a drunk at the top of the stairs in the dark. When you used the abbreviation before, that n, it was an intimate act, an adoring diminutive, as though to make the beloved compact enough to carry with you secretly. You always found me tall for a woman (too tall?) Now it's as though you want to avoid repeating my full name: Arnella. Nelli. nell. n. To deduct the name down to nothing. Nobody, no one, nowhere, nothing, nought, null, nil.

yes yes

The one thing you would never say in the act was *Yes!*—it was always *O no O no O no O no!* when you were getting close, and when I asked if it was because something was wrong, this "thing" was wrong, or was your pleasure (I would like to think so) intense to the point of pain, you went shy and said it was "just what came out—you know" (your favourite lazy phrase) "like when a song shows up in your head and you just, like, let it out?" I didn't press the point. I sensed you retreating into your separate memoir of intimate events. I didn't ask if that was what *always* "came out," or only with me. Separate memoirs, former loves. How crowded our bedrooms are these days. (Or not. Not my bedroom. Not these days). For over a century there was a tunnel extending from the crypt of the main cathedral here, down to the Hôtel-Dieu, the old Catholic hospital, so the priests could stay indoors in winter when they were called off to see sick parishioners or perform the last rites. A few weeks ago I read about it and for some reason kept wanting to tell you. Why not now. Forty years ago they decided the tunnel was becoming unsafe. They sealed it off at both ends, but the passageway is still there, thirty feet under Brock Street, totally dark, of course, and empty. Sometimes now when I'm alone it hits me.

reflect a little

Five days of this little reflecting. Here is what
gnaws me, besides the after-effects of five days
of little reflecting on your part and much waiting
on mine. What gnaws and haunts me is: whatever
passed through your mind in those five (plus) days,
all the stuff you decided not to voice, reconsidered,
revised, rejected then retrieved, reneged on again,
at last deleted. I want it back, the full census of your
reflections, a crammed CATscanful, all those references
to me, I can't accept they're gone, neural flickers like
email never sent or lost in transit somewhere in the
digital ether we're all adrift in now. Or: whispers of a
couple passing in that tunnel before it was sealed. A
pair of nuns, let's say, lovers on the down low, erotically
revved up by the proximity of illness, death. Death's
weirdly elating ultimacy. Did they have torches? A
medieval image, cinematic to the point of camp: dark
figures hunched, capes wafting, torches in hand,
flapping down limestone corridors propped with
timber stays for safety, as in a mine-shaft. Our lovers
must feel unnerved, even so. They are crossing so many
lines. The anxiety of the crime makes one notice other
dangers everywhere. And safety measures always seem

to whisper: *some day we will fail!* It feels safer where there are no measures. And either way, in their presence or absence, no safety.

i'm sorry

Sorry, maybe, because there *were* no reflections? You'd made up your mind? You're sorry that you stalled about breaking the news, is all? They say that from the bottom of a deep hole, you can see the stars shining even at noon. I never trust those little factlets from the *Globe*; still, it's good news for the dead.

and I *do* think it might be best

Italics mine. But even without the italics (it's my ethnic privilege to overuse them) your implication here is that *I made the suggestion in the first place!* Actually, of course, I did: "If you need me to pull back now, I will." Naturally I didn't mean it, though. Didn't want you to *accept*. Wanted you to say *O no O no O no O no!* What's more, *you must have known I didn't mean it*—you just pretended to take the words at face value to give yourself a convenient out. Lovers are the world's only honest people, according to certain poets and sages. Ho ho ho.

I'm nostalgic for the Salad Days, grad and postgrad in the late '70s and early '80s, York and UBC, when it was an article of faith (if not experience) in our circle that straight lovers, bourgeois lovers, were the only dishonest ones. *T[he] on/lie dys/honest ones*.

That stage of life when confidence depends on culprits.

Oh, to have both back.

i seem to need some space

But, but I thought we were bitter opponents of platitudes, you and I; we agreed that our love *was not like any other love* (italics mine, quote yours, email 64, line 17: I am now chief archivist of your intimacies), and to consecrate and, as you would say, "honour" this singularity, we agreed that we would never speak of our love in clichés. We smogged the air with exalted vows like that. Teenage summer lovers in a song by the Boss. So, maybe a return to cliché is a neatly symmetrical way to shut things down . . . to *deconsecrate* our love, the way they do with those churches whose flocks have died off or moved to Palm Beach, and the buildings are converted to meeting halls or museums or daycares. Ever wondered how they deconsecrate a cathedral? I really should know, after a quarter century in my field. (A century, one learns, is a small thing). A choir assembles for the last time, chanting in discord, an infernal chorus. At the altar a bishop exhausts the full roster of religious obscenities. The organist, wild-eyed, riffs on anthem-rock standards, Queen, Gary Glitter, The Sweet, as if playing at a hockey rink.

j, my j, you've *recanted*.
Shouldn't "recant" mean to sing again?

to hear my own breathing

If I woke in the night, the precious nights I had you here, I was always taken aback at how hard it was to detect your breaths. Even when you were deeply out (pretty much always) your breathing was delicate; once or twice I almost panicked, you know how the mind works at night, and there were always those footlights of unease around our meetings, fear of your husband interrupting our, uh, tutorial with a call, so that panic would feed on puny fears and several times I actually put the back of my hand to your open mouth to feel the breaths. Then my mouth next to yours to breathe them in. That close, I found you breathing, of course, calm and profound, with the faintest alto wheeze low in your chest, under your bare breasts, which were pillowed one over the other as you lay furled on your side. Your breath smelled fine, spicy, with a subtle finish of garlic and Syrah. Then one night it changed. That's how I knew we were coming to an end. More conventional signs had arisen as well—your canned laughter, diluted gaze, undilated pupils—but *that* was how I knew: the last two nights your breath turned unfamiliar in your sleep. Changes deep inside, where I couldn't reach. I wonder about the air in that blocked tunnel, after forty years of disuse. Is oxygen stable or does it deteriorate over time? I wouldn't know. Your husband would. Could toxic fumes have seeped in through the limestone? If the ends were unblocked tonight, could we still walk through it and breathe? How long does a closed-off tunnel remain a possible route?

always in dialogue

To you it may have felt that way. You're the one with other allegiances. (More of them, maybe, than I thought). A day came when I abandoned my latest stalled article to check email—still dial-up then—maybe thirty times, hoping for a reply. You must have been reflecting a little. Finally I just remained online, waiting. I answered a few other "urgent" emails that I'd left to ripen for days, maybe weeks. That took some time. I've never learned, like you, to crash out a reply, in lower-case, in the current electronic shorthand that I am still not used to—insulting!—though I see it all the time from my students :) Did those. Waited. Stared at the empty inbox and willed a message to appear. For quite some time I stuck it out. Funny, I've never once sat staring at the phone, though you would sometimes call me. Staring at a phone seems somehow goofier. A screen is meant to be stared at. Things are meant to appear there. Maybe I could *induce* you to write me. Eventually I took the modem cord and slunk the three flights down to the lobby and locked it in the morgue-like drawer of my mailbox. Came upstairs for a double Campari and soda. Left the cord down there for a good half hour.

i am sorry if this feels abrupt or my reasons feel vague, they just must be

Oh and another nice thing about email: you are always sitting down to read it. No more Puccini swoons, buckling to the floor with the farewell letter clinched in one hand, the other cupping the brow. Instead, you settle deeper in your chair. The world stops entering your mind through the senses. You've been sealed off with your obsession, and shame. *my reasons must be kept vague*. I always knew there were truths you wouldn't tell me, so I avoided entering certain corridors of inquiry; but there was also an implication, about the two of us, that we just *knew*— we UNDERSTOOD. William Burroughs said that gay love differs from straight love because a queer lover ("homosexual" was how he put it, I believe) always knows what the other is thinking and feeling, while a straight lover never does. Hmmm...Better that I did my thesis on Bloomsbury and Woolf, instead of (a quip over cocktails, long ago) Bloomsbury & the Beats: Points of Unexpected Comparison.

as i guess i implied

Didn't we make a pact never to do this sort of thing? To *guess* and *imply*? To become, in each other's sight, hazy at the margins by delivering half-truths? That's how people deconsecrate themselves, from human into something less. Spectres. Cyborgs. Didn't I mention this opinion? Not that you listened well, ever. Speaking of blockages. Consider the ears of the egotist...Now, as I listen, trying to peer through this blockage, I wonder if you are alone. There's your husband, of course, but he doesn't count. Two daughters. Neither do they. For the purpose of this madness only *somebody else* counts. (Especially if female.) You told me I was the first woman you had been with. Is there another now? Have I created a monster?

i have been asked to keep secrets

The cathedral's literature (I went and took one of their free tourist leaflets; lit a lampion for the hell of it) gives no clue as to how, or with what, the passageway was sealed.

i know you understand

See above under Burroughs, William.

you, after all, are one of my secrets

One of your . . . excuse me? I thought this was an exclusive engagement! Now I'm no longer your secret, I'm *one* of your secrets? Um, are your secrets a *clique* now? A *category*? A *women's collective*? All on the same level. . .Maybe your secrets should be more civil about this. Maybe they should all get *used* to one another. Your secrets are "all in this together". . .no rank, no priority, no hierarchy of closeness. . .it's a sorority, a full *democracy* of secrets!. . .The one exact thing that love isn't.

as you know yourself

Oh, I do. One of us had to end it. The question is: who began it, Janet? Another reference that dates me and, by omission, you. We have all the particulars. The year (2002). The season (summer). The place (Kingston). The course (Religious Imagery in Popular Culture and Contemporary Women's Fiction), and you in semi-attendance to steal time—admit it, finally, you're a dabbler, a summer slummer—away from your aphasic husband and colicky twins. When you went back to Winnipeg in the fall, I assumed it was over, but the thing wouldn't die. Since then I've propped everything on your annual holiday here in the Thousand Islands.

maybe a severing

New word for an old context. Feels more honest than "spend a little time apart," anyway. And honesty is what we all want at such times. But *severing*—there is a hard word. I'd never noticed the "severe" in it before. Or really heard the sound of it before. *SEVering*. The oiled blade sliding down to separate head from body with a blunt, chunky sound.

a temporary severing

Whew! For a minute there I thought it was permanent! As if it was in the very *nature* of severings to be that way. . .But a moment's reflection allows us to generate any number of counter-examples. In the fatal crash, the victim's spinal cord was *temporarily* severed. As the glaciers retreated, rising seawaters *temporarily* severed Asia from North America. Alas, it proved necessary to sever the miner's gangrenous limb *temporarily*. Somehow the bungee jumper's cord was severed in mid-leap—*but only temporarily!*

for both of you

You always wrote your emails fast, furtively, late at night or early in the morning, and there were always misspellings or little misprisions like this one. "Both of *us*," I assume you meant. You and me. Because there aren't two people hereabouts, in my world, my room. All the same. . .maybe you did half-mean that *I've* been as split apart as you. Between wanting to respect your family commitments and wanting you all to my lonesome? Nope: between wanting *not* to violate the current student-teacher protocol (which I always supported and still believe in and which the dying white males of the department, just them, allegedly, still flout when they can) and wanting to violate, repeatedly, you.

for everyone involved

Everyone! How did they get into this again? How I detest them! From the moment a love starts, Everyone is clamouring to get in, huffing and prodding, mobbing the door that a new couple seals fast and barricades—everyone trying to peep through, push through, leaving messages, making demands. I should have known Everyone would get to us. They always do. Over and over I've lived my life for those days before they do.

i am determined to get through this time

The ambiguity! It makes me insane! How many times have I been over this one, trying to uncrate it? You are determined to ride out this painful, severe time in your life? Or: you are determined, *this* time, to get through? Let it be the first option! Let it be that this hurts you as much as it hurts me. Let this not be yet another unacceptable revelation—that our affair wasn't your first of the kind. You said it was. Now, you might be saying there was another time and you *didn't* get through it—never got over her. (Or him). Other *times*? Who. Who. This vision of multitudes barging into your inbox, your bedroom, your body.

i will get in touch again when i feel i can

What's this if not a melodramatic way of saying, Don't call us, we'll call you? My people will call your people. My multitudes will call your solitude. . .but don't hold your breath. (Whatever remains in that sealed place). Cave exploration is something you always said you wanted to try out. I can hardly bare to use the correct, ridiculous term. Spelunking. I spelunk, you spelunk. We will spelunk. She had spelunked. So we'll go no more spelunking. Partly this is why I keep bringing up that sealed tunnel—not as some elaborate genital metaphor, but because I know you would be interested and maybe want to explore it. Count me out, though. Daredevils come in aerial or subterranean form. How many folks do you know who have both skydived and spelunked? Doesn't happen. When you would talk about spelunking, I would counter with skydiving, my own potential deathwish-hobby. We had to compromise on the earth's surface—on driving *really, really fast* those few times when we were far from everyone together. Rental cars are good for that: convertibles. A *Thelma and Louise* out-take, except people probably took me for your aunt, or duenna. Remember the highway into the Cypress Hills? How amazed you were that such committed flatness could collect itself into hills—small mountains, our ears popping as we drove—the way your life seemed to be climbing up from the plains of your comfortable present onto high ridges of possibility. . .

love always

But there's hope here, isn't there, there's not just a name, and not just "love"—no, it's "love always," even if there *is* the one conspicuous, crushing change, the absence of your usual starburst of xxxxxooooo's. Or xoxoxoxo. It always varied. I go back through the emails now (printed out, of course—there's a paper trail after all, sweetie, though you prudently avoided writing letters)—I pore over them again, studying, tabulating the details of the x and o firework-finale in all your emails, one hundred and fifty-eight in all, but especially the last twenty or so. I am trying to track the decline. How does the end enter? Where does it get in? In your most passionate note (I won't say email), right after the Cypress Hills Escapade, there were no less than ten x's and seven o's. (Why fewer o's than x's? Why *stint* like that on the o's? And what *are* x's and o's anyway? Kisses and embraces, embraces and kisses. We argued about which were which. To both of us it seemed obvious, a matter of common sense and common knowledge, and we were stunned, in a loving way, by the other's ignorance. You said, "O is the lips open for a deep kiss, X is the arms crossed over the embraced lover's back." Touched by this effort I replied, "Ingenious but wrong. O is the circle of the embracing lover's arms, X is the eye of the lover, the eyes, closed, X-ed out in the rapture of the kiss.")

Love as a game of noughts and crosses.

Nine emails before the end, I find *all my love, j, xxxooxx*. Again this marked privileging of x over o. (Five and three). Five messages before the end, *Love forever, j, xxxxoo*. (Four and two). Three messages before the end, o makes something of a comeback, outnumbering x for the first time in many missives, *Love, j, ooxxxooo*. In fact, the total number of signs here, eight, suggests if anything a strengthening of passion! Next, email 156, where o makes its final strong showing, *my love, j, ooxoo*—with the lone x almost lost among those still fervent hugs (or kisses???) Number 157, the second last, shows this tic-tac-toe showdown entering its endgame, although the salutation—*yours always, j, ox*—almost seems to cancel out that lack.

j

I'm to be spared the final humiliation. You'll remain j to me, not Janet-Marie. In signing off, you could have withdrawn that intimate, tiny link between us, that hook lodged in my heart, and keyed in your full name. You chose not to; something does remain unsevered. And after all, if the Greek in the labyrinth (you never remember the names), slowly unreeling his ball of yarn so he could find his way back, had accidentally cut the thread—maybe on a cornering wall where a sharp edge of stone jutted—he might have sensed it break and groped his way back in the darkness, feeling for the lost end, splicing the yarn, persevering. We're back in the tunnel, you see. Despite my fear, I think I would go down and explore it with you, if they ever opened it up again. I am drawn to a fantasy of fucking you there, maybe in a side tunnel or cul de sac, tugging you away from the tedious tour group with its silly costumed guide to make slow, wordless love in the kind of darkness people never really do it in. What would that be like? To have not the faintest glimpse or inkling of the one beside you, above you, below you? So the orgasm I'd give you, the way you liked it best, would star the gloom, seeming to project

on the walls a brief, grand, enveloping galaxy. There we
would be our own source of light. I don't want to see
anything now. Darkness is far from the worst. Your
note is very short. Worst is the whiteness of most of
the print-out under that j. So I've filled it and other
pages, your faithful annotator and emptied teacher,
with these notes, endnotes, that our dialogue not die.

Bill Howell
MANAGEMENT HAS DECIDED YOU MAY PREFER TO HEAR SOMETHING ELSE AT THIS TIME

The recurring nightmare centers on a long weekend inside a huge office complex. You used to work here but a lot's changed. They've agreed to return your ID fob, permitting you to attend a series of informal meetings. This is on an explicit understanding: you won't be having any original ideas. But dreams allow you extended periods without sleep or nourishment. If you can meet enough people, you'll earn enough points to get a new contract on Tuesday. Most of these people are stern women in purple culottes. Apparently they run the place. Food is catered, there's no direct contact with the outside world, nobody has a rollicking clue what season it is. Instead of speaking, everybody uses telepathic email. It feels like living in a bad movie except nobody's bothered to get the rights. Then you notice you're missing an arm again. As the place slowly consumes you, you realize: There's no _here_ here. You call home between meetings: "They've announced nobody has to pretend to read scripts anymore." Of course you're both being monitored to ensure quality control. *Having decided to kill things later*, a ghost on the line whispers, *the cat sleeps through Debussy.*

A.M. Klein
ANNUAL BANQUET: CHAMBRE de COMMERCE

And as the orators, rewarded roars, scored, soared, bored—
The man of capital:
You certainly have a wonderful country. Why don't you
Exploit it?

To which his neighbour and host
Seeking in pocket and pouch
Bosom and hip and thigh
At last produced it, bold and double-column.

> *Quebec: The place for industry*
> *Cheap power. Cheap labour.*
> *No taxes (first three years).*
> *No isms (forever).*

Verso, the guest beheld; and smiled:
Photograph of Mr. & Mrs. Damase Laberge

on the occasion of their 25th wedding anniversary,
surrounded by their children and grandchildren
to the number of thirty-two; from left to right...

O love which moves the stars and factories...

Stephen Leacock
MY FINANCIAL CAREER

When I go into a bank I get rattled. The clerks rattle me; the wickets rattle me; the sight of the money rattles me; everything rattles me.

The moment I cross the threshold of a bank and attempt to transact business there, I become an irresponsible idiot.

I knew this beforehand, but my salary had been raised to fifty dollars a month and I felt that the bank was the only place for it.

So I shambled in and looked timidly round at the clerks. I had an idea that a person about to open an account must needs consult the manager.

I went up to a wicket marked "Accountant." The accountant was a tall, cool devil. The very sight of him rattled me. My voice was sepulchral.

"Can I see the manager?" I said, and added solemnly, "alone." I don't know why I said "alone."

"Certainly," said the accountant, and fetched him.

The manager was a grave, calm man. I held my fifty-six dollars clutched in a crumpled ball in my pocket.

"Are you the manager?" I said. God knows I didn't doubt it.

"Yes," he said.

"Can I see you," I asked, "alone?" I didn't want to say "alone" again, but without it the thing seemed self-evident.

The manager looked at me in some alarm. He felt that I had an awful secret to reveal.

"Come in here," he said, and led the way to a private room. He turned the key in the lock.

"We are safe from interruption here," he said; "sit down." We both sat down and looked at each other. I found no voice to speak.

"You are one of Pinkerton's men, I presume," he said.

He had gathered from my mysterious manner that I was a detective. I knew what he was thinking, and it made me worse.

"No, not from Pinkerton's," I said, seeming to imply that I came from a rival agency.

"To tell the truth," I went on, as if I had been prompted to lie about it, "I am not a detective at all. I have come to open an account. I intend to keep all my money in this bank."

The manager looked relieved but still serious; he concluded now that I was a son of Baron Rothschild or a young Gould.

"A large account, I suppose," he said.

"Fairly large," I whispered. "I propose to deposit fifty-six dollars now and fifty dollars a month regularly."

The manager got up and opened the door. He called to the accountant.

"Mr. Montgomery," he said unkindly loud, "this gentleman is opening an account, he will deposit fifty-six dollars. Good morning."

I rose. A big iron door stood open at the side of the room. "Good morning," I said, and stepped into the safe.

"Come out," said the manager coldly, and showed me the other way.

I went up to the accountant's wicket and poked the ball of money at him with a quick convulsive movement as if I were doing a conjuring trick.

My face was ghastly pale.

"Here," I said, "deposit it." The tone of the words seemed to mean, "Let us do this painful thing while the fit is on us."

He took the money and gave it to another clerk. He made me write the sum on a slip and sign my name in a book. I no longer knew what I was doing. The bank swam before my eyes.

"Is it deposited?" I asked in a hollow, vibrating voice.

"It is," said the accountant.

"Then I want to draw a cheque."

My idea was to draw out six dollars of it for present use. Someone gave me a chequebook through a wicket and someone else began telling me how to write it out. The people in the bank had the impression that I was an invalid millionaire. I wrote something on the cheque and thrust it in at the clerk. He looked at it.

"What! are you drawing it all out again?" he asked in surprise. Then I realized that I had written fifty-six instead of six. I was too far gone to reason now. I had a feeling that it was impossible to explain the thing. All the clerks had stopped writing to look at me.

Reckless with misery, I made a plunge.

"Yes, the whole thing."

"You withdraw your money from the bank?"

"Every cent of it."

"Are you not going to deposit any more?" said the clerk, astonished.

"Never."

An idiot hope struck me that they might think something had insulted me while I was writing the cheque and that I had changed my mind. I made a wretched attempt to look like a man with a fearfully quick temper.

The clerk prepared to pay the money.

"How will you have it?" he said.

"What?"

"How will you have it?"

"Oh"—I caught his meaning and answered without even trying to think—"in fifties."

He gave me a fifty-dollar bill.

"And the six?" he asked dryly.

"In sixes," I said.

He gave it me and I rushed out.

As the big door swung behind me I caught the echo of a roar of laughter that went up to the ceiling of the bank. Since then I bank no more. I keep my money in cash in my trousers pocket and my savings in silver dollars in a sock.

John B. Lee
CRUEL WITH BOOKS

I told this good man,
my uncle's brother,
when he asked: "I'm a writer."
I watched the colour drain
from his face
like a cloth that could not hold the dye
and his shoulders fall in his shirt
his wrists lose their grip in the cuffs
as if in speaking I had conjured
for this gentle farmer
all those years his schoolmasters
had been cruel with books.

All those mysteries they had used to mock him
with the awful misery of certain letter-clever men
he'd gladly left behind.

And I wanted to say,
"I'm not the one
who'd wield the written word
against your world
or hold this poem's worth a weapon
to separate our hearts."
But I see, it is too late for us.
Still I want impossible communities of men
to lay aside their unimportant hurts
and in the rustle of corn
or the rustle of unwrapping Sunday shirts
to marry silk and rust
and find the rose in the box is still a rose
that wants water
and the refrigerated apple
sometimes remembers the tree.

Seymour Mayne
FOR THE DENTIST WHO EXTRACTED MY LAST WISDOM TOOTH

Gone, it still gnaws the jaw's bone—
Nemetic reminder where stitches are sewn.

Only the law of Moses gives me sooth:
Next time, sir, it's a tooth for a tooth.

Bruce Meyer
DEATH AND THE HUMAN RESOURCES MANAGER

It came slowly like a morning memo
or a burst of corporate inspiration.
The telephone rang. The rolodex, slow
to respond, offered no networking.
It was as if the entire operation
had been outsourced. He was asking

a question at the time. The answer
had something to do with attrition,
an overlooked redundancy. Sure
of its legalities, the silence battled
to be heard. That was how policy
came down. The matter settled,
Life went out to lunch with Reality.

SUCCESS

—for Ray Robertson

When I die I want to be remembered
as someone who succeeded in life;
and the more I try, the quicker I approach
that successful end. In triplicate, strife

bids me fill out its requisite forms, one
for accounting, one for the files,
and the last for the system. When done,
only the fire-breathing system smiles.

Please name an award for pointless
dedication after me and present it
to the next overachiever who climbs
the mountain of paperwork and shit

in the pursuit of excellence. A wall
is not an obstacle to a bricklayer.
A door is an opportunity, not an exit.
Remember the fool dragonslayer.

Shane Neilson
NO ILL EFFECTS

I doctor like Charon tends to his staff;
on your eyes the aureus as tumour.
My heart is a weighscale, gravity the laugh

at death. Drink deep; you will drink. Quaff
like Galen and his sense of humor;
I've doctored like Charon tends to his staff.

Be glad he didn't beat you with it. Be half-
sad; I hear it's the perfect weight of cure.
My heart a weighscale, gravity the laugh.

My stethoscope opines on your behalf,
says: it's not all that bad. *Stethy, I am sure*, for
I doctor like Charon tends to his staff.

What goes up comes down six feet. Sacrificial calf,
you are in my clinic's sterile abattoir, where
my heart is the weighscale, gravity the laugh.

I'll make the first incision with a gaff
that waits patiently. I bait the lure.
I doctor like Charon tends to his staff;
My heart is a weighscale, gravity the laugh.

John Oughton
ODE TO THE TD BANK

I have lived at the same address so long
that mail is slid through my mouth
and strangers grasp my hand to open
the door. Although I remain unmarried
all women work for me and offer up
their assets. The stars of the sky
I keep as jewels in my eye's vault.
I sleep in stocks and drink nothing
but bonded.

In fact limestone banks
chase me along the street trailing tapes
and begging for my magic valve kiss
to release the pressure of their
respectability. Most of all
I ask for money because I do not
even remotely need it, but only intend
to honour that minor art form:
the won loan
which holds up all Bay Street.

P.K. Page
THE STENOGRAPHERS

After the brief bivouac of Sunday,
their eyes, in the forced march of Monday to Saturday,
hoist the white flag, flutter in the snow-storm of paper,
haul it down and crack in the mid-sun of temper.

In pause between the first draft and the carbon
they glimpse the smooth hours when they were children—
the ride in the ice-cart, the ice man's name,
the end of the route and the long walk home;

remember the sea where floats at high tide
were sea marrows growing on the scatter-green vine
or spools of grey toffee, or wasps' nests on water;
remember the sand and the leaves of the country.

Bell rings and they go and the voice draws their pencil
like a sled across snow; when its runners are frozen
rope snaps and the voice then is pulling no burden
but runs like a dog on the winter of paper.

Their climates are winter and summer—no wind
for kites of their hearts—no wind for a flight;
a breeze at the most, to tumble them over
and leave them like rubbish—the boy-friends or blood.

In the inch of the noon as they move they are stagnant.
The terrible calm of the noon is their anguish;
The lip of the counter, the shapes of the straws
like icicles breaking their tongues, are invaders.

Their beds are their oceans—salt water of weeping
the waves that they know—the tide before sleep;
and fighting to drown they assemble their sheep
in columns and watch them leap desks for their fences
and stare at them with their own mirror-worn faces.

In the felt of the morning the calico-minded,
sufficiently stretched, inserted papers, hit keys,
efficient and sure as their adding machines;
yet they weep in the vault, they are taut as net curtains
the pin men of madness in marathon trim
race round the track of the stadium pupil.

Molly Peacock
OUR ROOM

I tell the children in school sometimes
why I hate alcoholics: my father was one.
"Alcohol" and "disease" I use, and shun
the word "drunk" or even "drinking," since one time
the kids burst out laughing when I told them.
I felt as though they were laughing at me.
I waited for them, wounded, remem-
bering how I imagined they'd howl at me
when I was in grade 5. Acting drunk
is a guaranteed screamer, especially
for boys. I'm quiet when I sort the junk
of my childhood for them, quiet so we
will all be quiet, and they can ask what
questions they have to and tell about what
happened to them, too. The classroom becomes
oddly lonely when we talk about our homes.

Lauralee Proudfoot
OVERLOAD (A RICTAMETER)

Process
Information.
Bureaucracy often
Removes logic from the process—
Turns everything into hoop jumping.
Jump! Jump! Higher and quicker now!
Now wait patiently—wait...
And wait more for
Process.
Red tape
Tangled and balled
Mess of incompetence
Blamed—again—on technology
No need to take responsibility
Of course it is not your fault, no
The computers, the rules
Conspire—create
Red tape.

Other
Technology
Turns those that do not fit
Into the boxes on the forms
Different, talented, gifted, or not
Into problems. Square pegs in round holes
Don't belong in data.
They become the
Other.

Julie Roorda
WORDS MISREAD ON THE LIPS

Then the faces of all the dead
appeared in the mirrored windows
of the sky-scrapers.

At first these were mistaken,
for forgotten psychiatric patients,
until people recognized their own

dead and cleared the nightly crop
of smashed birds from the ground
below to pay some respect.

A brave few ventured inside, flapped
their arms, hoping to be seen through
the visage of the dead.

The dead could be seen to speak
but were not heard. The deaf
suddenly in demand. Disputes arose.

Did she say bury or marry? Ashes
or hatches? Did he say love
or life or leave?

Malcontent, the living chose
to get back to business, the evidence
dismissed as ambiguous, at best.

Robert Service
FIVE-PER-CENT

Because I have ten thousand pounds I sit upon my stern,
And leave my living tranquilly for other folks to earn.
For some procreative way that isn't very clear,
Ten thousand pounds will breed, they say, five hundred every year.
So as I have a healthy hate of economic strife,
I mean to stand aloof from it the balance of my life.
And yet with sympathy I see the grimy son of toil,
And heartily congratulate the tiller of the soil.
I like the miner in the mine, the sailor on the sea,
Because up to five hundred pounds they sail and mine for me.
For me their toil is taxed unto that annual extent,
According to the holy shibboleth of Five-per-cent.

So get ten thousand pounds, my friend, in any way you can,
And leave your future welfare to the noble Working Man.
He'll buy you suits of Harris tweed, an Airedale and a car;
Your golf clubs and your morning *Times*, your whisky and cigar.
He'll cosily install you in a cottage by a stream,
With every modern comfort, and a garden that's a dream.
Or if your tastes be urban, he'll provide you with a flat,
Secluded from the clamour of the proletariat.

With pictures, music, easy chairs, a table of good cheer,
A chap can manage nicely on five hundred pounds a year.
And though around you painful signs of industry you view,
Why should you work when you can make your money work for you?

So I'll get down upon my knees and bless the Working Man,
Who offers me a life of ease through all my mortal span,
Whose loins are lean to make me fat, who slaves to keep me free,
Who dies before his prime to let me round the century;
Whose wife and children toil in turn until their strength is spent,
That I may live in idleness upon my five-per-cent.
And if at times they curse me, why should I feel the blame?
For in my place I know that they would do the very same.
Aye, though they hoist a flag that's red on Sunday afternoon,
Just offer them ten thousand pounds and see them change their tune.
So I'll enjoy my dividends and live my life with zest,
And bless the might men who first—*invented interest.*

Adam Sol
CITY SONG

Who's seen the phantom boy
        who used to drum pennies against metal gratings
                down here by the switching station?

Where could he be, now that I finally
        have something to show him,
                after months of marching past

on my way to strategy meetings and lunches?
        I used to shrug
                at his pathetic entreaties,

suggesting that I had nothing to give him that day,
        not today,
                and the shrug satisfied both of us.

He would smile and say, "Nice day," or "Cold one,"
        and I pretended to take that for
                a metaphysical forgiveness.

In this way we achieved an understanding,
        a sort of communion between men,
                an agreement to accept

that we would never touch each other.
        But here I am,
                I have walked this strip of sidewalk

for two hours in search of him
        because I think I found his dog behind my building,
                half buried in leaf oatmeal.

Bones so thin they could be syringes.

Raymond Souster
THIS DAY

You can tell
by the strong
and early sunrise
that this day
really means business.

Robert Sward
MILLIONAIRE

—Grandpa Max, 1860-1958

1. His inventions

Born in 1860, Austro-Hungarian immigrant,
inventor of a cap to keep the fizz
in seltzer bottles, a refinement to the machine gun,
and a metal Rube Goldberg bookmark
       sold with a diagram and user manual,
Grandpa made big money speculating,
buying and selling tenements.
In the 1920s, offered stock in a start-up selling
flavored water and cocaine, he turned it down. "Coca
Cola," he spat.
"Vhat dreck! Who'd buy?"

2. His economies

Lean, stiff-necked, pack-a-day smoker
with a fondness for syrupy wine, he wouldn't own a car,
used public transportation;
and, rather than buy toilet paper,
blackened his ass with yesterday's *Chicago Tribune*.

Grandpa never left a restaurant
—"vegetable soup, roll, glass of water"—
without pocketing a few cellophane-wrapped crackers
        "for later."

At six, I got my first lesson in thrift.
Grandpa with a smoker's cough:
"Cough into four corners of hanky,
like this—
four coughs minimum—
before you dirty up the middle."
End of lesson.

3. His curses

Late summer afternoons, partaking of Mogen David
("Shield of David") wine,
he orbited the living room, sonofabitching
the government
                and Democrats with no sense,
Franklin and Eleanor Roosevelt, "betrayers of the rich,
and they stole my patent, too."

God damning union leaders, *schnorrers,*
the United Mine Workers,
the AFL and CIO,
"Stand 'em up against a wall.
Shoot 'em, shoot the sons-a-bitches."

4. His secret to health and long life

Old Testament Moses,
cigarette and drink in hand,
white mustache, gray beard, pacing, pacing,
"God" (it was a prayer after all),
"damn" (the patriarch calling down wrath),
"son-a-bitch, son-a-bitch."
The last of his great inventions,
five syllables to God's four ("Let there be light"),
but good enough.
And that is how he'd breathe, cursing
—head back, chin up—everyone who, he figured,
had somehow cost him money.
"God damn son-a-bitch, God damn son-a-bitch!" he'd rage,
miraculously cured of whatever ailed him.

George Swede
WINDOWLESS OFFICE

windowless office
a fly buzzes against
my glasses

*

as the professor speaks
only his bald spot
is illuminated

*

train to a ghost town
the historian asks to sit
facing backwards

*

Today at work
I saw the complexity
of labour vs. management—

a lake gull flies silently
through the snowfall

*

Department meeting:
while mouths utter business
the eyes ripple with
someone sailing, someone fishing
someone drowning

*

     working late
I meet my loneliness
  in the long hallway

*

pontificating colleague...
the mosquito on his arm
swells contentedly

A LOCAL HISTORY OF HOPE

Today on the corner
a doughnut shop
where only a week ago was
a take-out pizza parlor
and a year earlier
a stationery supplier
and two years antecedent
a comic book emporium
and four years prior
a tuxedo rental outlet
and five years preceding
a boutique
and seven years previous
a men's clothing store
and eleven years before that
bare hardwood floors
and ivory-white walls
gleaming with promise
and in the large window
the first sign
NEW RETAIL SPACE FOR RENT
      THRIVING LOCATION

H. Masud Taj
THE DOMAIN OF INBETWEEN

It is the season
Of digging into the earth
Sowing seeds, houses.
The seed that decides
Resides out of sight, below
The earth pondering
What it is to bask
In the sun, to feel the breeze
The sky's curvature
Exposed to all eyes,
The insider's intense gaze
To be and not flinch.

No storm can uproot
Submerged formations of stone
Sprouting foundations.
Lightning cracks the sky
Foundation breaks surface
The plinth sets the stage:
A site for healing
Rift between earth and sky
The stage is empty.

To descend with grace
Is the way of all raindrops
Till they fall on stage
Only to scatter.
What are explosions but flowers
Blossoming quickly.
Will the floor recall
When dispossessed of its sky
How rains celebrate?

To ascend with grace
Is the way of all columns,
To build is to grow.
Defoliated trees
Memories of branches, leaves
Some beyond recall.
Who can tell how deep
Columns plunge into the earth
To withstand the sky.
To be a column
Is to cultivate patience
While staking shadows.

Beams are but columns
Dreaming branches, reaching out
To other branches.
When columns and beams

Dream together, leaving earth
Soaring as an arch
To think is to fly
Transcending beams and columns
With stones and stillness.

Did you not wonder
With such flights into the sky
Would the stones return?

Stones in full flight freeze
Relish anti-gravity
Leaf and butterfly.
When stones taste the sky
They return home to earth
For a little while
Arches recall
Arrival and departure
In a single sweep
Tracing lips that frame
Mouth open in disbelief
At such momentum.

What can they enclose
When walls proceed beyond plinth
To watch a tree grow.
Walls know how to wait;

Dwelling is a lingering
Waiting the return.
Trees know how to spread
Branches, branching into tongues
As so many leaves
Chanting earthian hymns
That ascend as sky descends
In consummation.

The bird that alights
Fans out its structural wings,
The feathers are still.
Like a self styled sky
Simulating horizons,
The roof reposes;
The house reconciles
Roots that clutch, wings that soar
Between earth and sky.

What is it to roof?
What can house that which houses,
That which embraces.
Resting on shadows
On wings of cantilevers
On a grounded pledge;
No gaze can trespass
Where earth and sky intersect

The roofs cutting edge;
The line of cease fire
Is the distant horizon
Where all roofs spring from.

Does the view not change
With the way arches perform
On that which is seen?
What does the arch frame
The view within or without?
The shade or the sun?
Healing distances
Is the way of leaping stones,
Rainbows across time.
Will the dew linger
When the leaf begins to turn
And the sun returns?

To linger, to dwell
In the neighborhood of death
Where all life takes place.
The snail's epitaph
Is the form he leaves behind,
Shell is memory.
And then who can tell
Between the snail and the shell
Dweller and dwelling.

To be in that space
To be in treasury
Of all that happened.

Sleepwalkers beware
Dwelling is all pervasive
Dweller all aware
Where to change levels
Is an act of commitment
Unleashing stairways
That defy railings.
House is never logical
Logic dwells in it.
Do not take chances
Where right angles fear to tread
Through squeezed doors and stairs.

All places take place
Or are places arrived at
When you least expect.
Angles do not dwell
Where everything has its place
Where does the wind go?
And where do shadows?
All angles are full of them
Dreaming of nightfall.

Where do trees belong
In blind darkness of deep soil?
With sun-blinded leaves?
Could the earth foretell,
Could the vast sky imagine
Where all paths converge
There the house presides!
The hill circumambulates,
Flowers spiral open
To a redefined
Sky that locates its bearings
Where the house resides.

Where does it begin?
When does it stop becoming?
Will it ever be?
The dream of the house
Is to entice the dreamer
To linger a while
That which was within
Is no longer a secret
But an oasis.
To see is to touch
But to be touched is to see
For the very first time.

Archeological
Glass cut and stacked in strata
Opaques to reveal
The yearning of all
That is invisible to
Become visible.
What was transparent
Is as translucent as mist
That fills the valleys.
Ancient light filters
Into rooms behind glass veils
Moonlight on water.

House is the mirror
Full of everything it sees
The forest outside.
Inside the forest
You come upon a clearing
Courtyard among trees.

Courtyard is silence
To talk about the courtyard
Is to break the spell.

When the center recedes
Leaving its absence behind
With its own heartbeat,
The house remains poised
In between two outsides
Where leaves hold their breath.
Some places become
Sites of possibilities
Where trees yearn to be.

Diagonal slashes
The rectangle into two
Triangles open.
The pathway turns to
Subterranean chambers
Underneath gardens.
Roots metamorphose
Into fertile grounds that sprout
Grass and domes of glass
Ringed with wine bottles
Intoxicated with light
Sunflowers celebrate

Form follows fiction,
Stepping across the threshold
The skeptic believes
The visual logic
Of virtual reality
Is it as you see?
Where does the house dwell?
The domain of inbetween
Where we always are.

To blend with the earth
To stand out against the sky
To transcend seasons.
To be is to dwell
To preside and to reside
Simultaneously.

To speak of the house
Is to wipe the mouth with words
So that it may speak.

Priscila Uppal
A REFERRAL

The dentist stole my teeth.
The optician burned my eyes.
The nutritionist emptied my fridge.
The gynecologist kidnapped my thighs.

The reflexologist misaligned my chakras.
The dermatologist boycotted my skin.
The psychologist sliced my childhood.
The oral surgeon punched my chin.

The oncologist gave me cancer.
The anaestitician misread my chart.
The frenologist shrunk my left brain.
The cardiologist attacked my heart.

Now I am but a case study.
My file is up for review.
Today we rearrange the suffering.
Tomorrow I'll be healing you.

MY OVIDIAN EDUCATION

After a long respite in the lavatory trying to get my head around
how so many twenty-somethings and a few older ladies
can think of nothing better to say after a presentation on Paul Celan
than "That was deep I guess, was this guy gay?"
I emerge with a blazer as white as chalk dust
and a pencil case as dour as a coffin and leaning into the mirror
discover I have aggravatingly beautiful cheeks and deep-set
Firestone tire eyes but a nose with a hook as sharp
as the old hermit in my Renaissance plates dictionary. Under
the neon lights of the chemistry hallway, eating an orange,
a banana, and a box of SunMaid raisins, I would sell my soul
for a student worth Platonizing about and a stack of letters
urging me to adulterize my standards just this once
and leave them all sitting there without a second act after intermission
to their exercizes on metaphor and lists of ten questions
to ask of their poems, including "Why should anyone but you
care about what you've written?" and dive off the top
of academe's steeple cracking my nose on the concrete
waiting for the one with the shiniest apple to sing me and Paul back to life.

MY STOMACH FILES A LAWSUIT

I know I've done wrong.
Negligence, I'm sure it
will be called.

I have violated the terms
of our initial agreement.
Property must switch hands.
Accounts have come due.

My liver and spleen
have received subpoenas.
They can't wait to talk out
of turn, to bury me.
Treachery has been building
for years.

My stomach has hired
a high-profile lawyer who threatens
to take me for all I'm worth.
I'm baffled by what becomes
of old friendships.

There was a time we might
have settled out of court;
shaken hands, exchanged signatures,
and parted ways. But not now.
Not after the endless editorials.

The court sketch artist
has her hands full. Though I should
be contemplating my defense,
my eyes are glued to her
pointed black nibs, recreating
our broken promises, our hunger,
in a few dark strokes.

Halli Villegas
THE PATH

Julie stepped off the subway and began to walk underground to her latest temp job. She's been doing temp work for five years now because her childhood fitted her out for absolutely nothing. She knows that it is not the done thing these days to blame your past or your equally blameless parents for any lack of future success, but really what did a childhood spent reading, eating Kraft Dinner and watching Love Boat while your parents are out doing *Waiting for Godot* at the community theatre and having affairs with their fellow thespians, suit you for? Not a whole hell of a lot. *And let's not even get started on genetics* she thinks, handily slipping in and out among the commuters that fill the walkways of this underground path that links all the business centers of the city, *that terrible overbite of my mother's that she never got fixed*.

The Path, which is what these underground walkways are called, is filled with restaurants and stores. It connects miles of the city in the downtown core, office buildings, banks, and malls. Higher up there's light, in the lobbies of office complexes, the main level of malls, but down here it is all artificial. The light is aquatic, diffuse, and everything is given a sort of dreamy quality. There are plants in strategic areas near elevators and stairwells. Once Julie saw the people who care for them hunching among them, doing things with hoses and spray bottles and buckets. She wonders how the plants can live without light, real light day in and day out, and wonders if they are given some sort of special vitamin to aid their sunless growth.

There were birds that lived in the path. They flew in through open doors on the ground floor and never left. They were lost, or confused, or maybe they just adapted to their situation. They ate the crumbs that were left behind in the food courts, hid in plants or else soared up and around the skylights on the lobby floors of the office buildings. Sometimes Julie would see one hopping around among the crowds hurrying to and from work and wonder if the birds felt the same sense of purpose, did they feel they belonged in the rush of living that flowed through the underground paths and up into the city?

No, they are just birds, all they think about is eating and propagating the species. Don't be so dramatic Julie.

Just past a rubber plant and some spider ferns Julie takes the elevator to the offices of Marvel and Harvey, the international design firm. Marv and Harv as they are called by the firm itself, trying to give themselves a cool non-corporate image. It's a weeklong gig, paying fourteen an hour for receptionist work, but requires absolutely no effort what so ever. Julie is the perfect temp, serviceable, dependable and expendable. Of course she cultivates vague artistic pretensions. You can't be a temp admin with out some sort of mandate about not wanting to cramp your creative output with a full time job. She crochets things, most recently berets with carrots dangling from the brim, and has put out a few issues of a zine cunningly illustrated and hand sewn with tooth floss where she rants about things like the death of Mr. Rogers. Julie varies her work description to people she meets on temp jobs, sometimes she says she's textile artist, other times she says she's a writer, a conceptualist poet to be exact, in case anyone asks her what she has written. That's why her agency puts her in placements that have creative overtones, even if all she'll be doing is answering phones. She's worked off and on for Marv and Harv for about three years, in all their different branches. She practices her phone greeting on the way up the elevator to the office, "Good afternoon Marv and Harv, how can I help you? Marv and Harv, how may I direct your call? Marv and Harv, please hold." Everyone else in the elevator ignores her, most of them are looking at their Blackberries and she is whispering.

Two hipsters in Buddy Holly glasses wearing grass green grandfather cardigans with Marv and Harv embroidered on them in white script, holding bright pink balloons greet her as she gets off the elevator. They are larger then life, with unsmiling, rather shocked expressions on their faces despite the logo "Let Our Ideas Take You Up and Away." *That's Marv and Harv all right, hipper then life.*

Julie hasn't been back here to the head office since it's redo.

The reception area is all glass and grey walls, cabinets with no handles that are a bitch to use because they only open the tiniest bit when you push them on their secret spot and then you have to try to ease your fingers in there with out scratching the finish in order to get anything out. Leather arm chairs, bowl of fruit, two TVs permanently tuned to CP 24, and worst of all a pod espresso machine.

Julie gave a long shudder, *oh god was she going to have to make coffee?* The reception area is empty. Usually an HR person comes down to meet with her and give her a passcard, but perhaps today there is a disgruntled employee holding them hostage, waving a gun around while they cower under desks.

Julie can't find the reception desk. There used to be a regular reception desk, blond wood, imposing, now, nothing. She looks around the slickster space, notices another bowl of fruit on the counter under a sign that says "Let us Grow Your Business Organically." Just as Julie is beginning to feel a little wave of panic *did I get the day wrong,* she sees tucked in the corner a two-foot by two-foot glass shelf attached to the wall. There is a computer on it and a phone but nothing else. No personal pictures, no pen cup, nothing. There is a Marv and Harv glass design award on a shelf above the desk, but that's it. Julie wonders how Marci, the receptionist that has been with the company for twenty years, feels about her designed desk. *Organically, does she feel her role has been organically enhanced?* Julie sits down at the desk and calls Lacey, her temp agency boss.

"Hey Julie, how's it going?"

"Fine, but no one was here to meet me."

"That's weird, give Carol in HR a call, they're probably in an interview or something."

"Lacey, did Marci tell you about the new desk they gave her?"

"Oh God yes, Marci's mad as hell about the

shelf thing. She thinks they want to squeeze her out so they can get someone sexy and young. Marci says they'll have to fire her before she quits."

"And they have a pod espresso maker out here."

"Ooh fancy schmancy. Has anyone asked you to make coffee?"

"Not yet, but I have a feeling they will."

"Well call if there are any problems and hang in there, its only for two weeks."

Julie hangs up the phone. She tries Carol in HR but can't get her. So she leaves a message on her voice mail, then she boots up Mah Jongg on her computer screen. When she first started Marv and Harv, she was told she couldn't read a book, no matter how slow it was. She had to give the appearance of working, at least looking at a computer screen. She takes the first two seasons tiles off the top of the pile and settles in for the afternoon.

Three days later the espresso maker comes into play. Camilla, Dick Marvell's personal assistant storms into the reception area. Camilla is a highstrung redhead. She wears her riotous red curls gelled and pulled severely back with a clip, no make up on her rolling washed out blue eyes and very thin lips, and has a nose that looks as if she is permanently smelling something distasteful.

"Oh God, Dick wants a latte, do you know how to use this thing?" Camilla begins to fumble with the pod machine, taking out cups and pitchers to froth milk, "Marci never lets me make Dick's lattes, she doesn't want me to touch the machine."

Reluctantly Julie gets up from her chair. She has never been a coffee aficionado and while she can handle a Mr. Coffee, espresso machines always leave her feeling inadequate. She appreciates Marci's power play. Together she and Camilla fumble with the machine. They manage to place the pod in the proper receptacle, but when they foam the milk it shoots all over and Julie has to go to the kitchen to get a J-cloth to wipe it up. Camilla takes it from her and wipes down every surface within a three foot radius of the machine, even in places where foam couldn't possibly have splattered. Julie manages to get the foaming under control and Camilla carefully pours the coffee into the cup. She looks into and says "I wish I could get a little heart on top like those fancy Italian places. Dick would be so impressed."

As she picks up the cup to go back to her office Dick Marvell storms into the lobby. He's tall with squinty blue eyes and is wearing jeans, a Stetson and sheepskin jacket. Apparently he thinks that Marlboro man is the hip corporate look for CEOs.

"Is that my coffee? Never mind, you were too slow. Lunch meeting and confirm that service to the airport for tomorrow." He strides out, as if he is going to check the fences.

Camilla stands very straight. She takes a sip of the latte.

Julie leans on the counter. "Hey Camilla, how does Marci stand it without a desk."

Startled Camilla turns to Julie, "Marci? She doesn't sit, she's the receptionist. She walks around the reception area."

"All day?"

"Its her job." Camilla leaves the empty cup on the counter for Julie to clean up.

On Monday Julie nearly breaks her neck coming out of the subway. She steps on a religious pamphlet and slips. The pamphlet has the Virgin on the cover and says Her Eyes Implore You in vivid red lettering. Someone has scattered them everywhere in the subway station. Julie gives the pamphlet a vicious kick and it sticks to her foot. She has to drag her boot along the station's tiles until it de-sticks. As she passes through the underground passages to the elevators for Marv and Harv she notices the homeless girl holding open the glass doors into the concourse. There are always homeless people holding open the doors for commuters for change. Julie is amazed at the business people who grandly sweep through the open door without even a glance at the person holding it open. Personally she will never go through a held open door because she doesn't carry change and is of two minds as to whether it is doing the person begging a favour or not to give them some odd bits of change from a linty pocket. She thinks it is probably better to give to charities, but she can't afford to. So she scrupulously opens her own doors. Today the girl holding open the door can't be more then eighteen. She has slanted eyes like a cat's in a startling green, and long ash blond hair. Her face is cat-like as well, small chin, wide cheekbones. She is dressed in a dirty parka and there is a smell of urine and cigarettes hanging over her. But for all that she is pretty, she could be a model if she was washed and clothed properly. *Why is she here, drugs? Must be drugs. She's so pretty, she could have been anything.* The girl sees Julie staring, she grins. Her teeth are missing in the front and what teeth are left are brown and cracked. Her mouth is a black hole opening in front of Julie, it seems as if her face is closer, so that she can smell the girl's breath, foetid and wet.

"Spare some change miss?"

Julie steps back, "No, no sorry."

"You'll be sorry when you're dead." The girl hisses at Julie. Julie hurries away not looking over her shoulder. The girl's smell seems to cling to her.

The first thing she does at Marv and Harv is go into the bathroom and wash her hands with the Savon de Marseilles soap they keep in there. Across the mirror is a sticker that says: Be the Change You Wish to See in the World. Keep Thinking Creatively! Julie bends over the sink and rinses her mouth out; she wishes she had thought to bring a toothbrush with her.

The next day Camilla hurries into the reception area and begins to make Dick's latte, she has the knack of it now and Julie feels sorry for Marci, having lost her sovereignty over the espresso machine. Camilla is chatty, in a good mood because Dick is in the office all day and keeping her hopping.

"You know Dick said my lattes are as good as Marci's. He's off to Washington next week, so I've been making all his arrangements. If the limo service calls, please put them through to my line directly. It's a new service, so I am not sure if they will have picked up on my extension number." Camilla looks at her watch, "Oh God Dick has those meetings in an hour and I still have to make sure the PowerPoint is set up and he has his hard copy. Can you make sure the main boardroom is clean and that there is a pitcher of water on both ends of the table? You know you really should be checking to see if the chairs are pushed in and the tables are cleared after every meeting. It is part of your job description and Dick hates it when the boardrooms are messy when he has meetings." Camilla rushes out, still muttering. Julie sighs and goes into the main boardroom. There is a gold star on the door. All the rooms have cutesy designators. This room is the Gold Star for Effort boardroom, and then there is the Kazamm boardroom whose sticker is the word Kazamm in a cartoon speech bubble in Comic Sans serif. Julie's particular favorite is The Rocket Man room whose insignia is a giant stylized rocket with sparkly flames coming out of it. Julie wonders if they got permission from Elton John to use the phrase. She almost wants to turn them in; maybe they'd get sued. She pulls the leather boardroom chairs into place, wondering why they couldn't just push them in when they are done with their meeting. She cleans up the empty paper cups and candy wrappers. Now the boardroom is ready for Dick.

About three o'clock that afternoon a man walks into the reception area. He is tall with dark hair slicked back and very deep blue eyes that match his tie. The contrast between his white dress shirt collar and the black and white of his face makes him look like an old fashioned advertisement for Arrow collars. His black suit is faultless. Despite herself Julie stands up.

"Welcome to Marv and Harv. Can I help you?"

The man grins at her with even white teeth. "I'm here to see that old reprobate Dick. He knows I'm coming."

"Can I get you a coffee or anything?"

"You mean one of those fancy espresso drinks Dick is so fucking proud of? Don't bother. It's still swill. You can only get the real stuff in Italy."

"I'll call Dick."

"Never mind, he's expecting me. I'll just go through." The man starts to move past her. For one panicky minute Julie is afraid she'll get in trouble, then she thinks *fuck it, I'm just the temp* and sits back down at her desk The man stops and looks at her.

"Is that your desk?" He's laughing. "Squeezing you out huh?"

Still laughing he moves on.

"I'm just the temp." Julie says, but he ignores her and goes through the glass doors into the offices.

She blushes and counts on her fingers how much longer she has before she is out, as far away from Marv and Harv as she can get.

On Wednesday as she rides the subway to work she overhears two girls talking. They are in their twenties, dressed in the uniform of administrative assistants everywhere. Cheap two piece suit from Smart Set or Style & Co. The shirt, a glossy burgundy or blue or green, made to look like silk, but with a sheen that proclaims pure poly rayon. These shirts are oddly sexy, with long pointed collars, and buttons that start at the bra, sometimes there is ruching across the breasts. They are practical; the shirt can be worn at the club, or for drinks after work. Completing the look are black tights and pumps that have the leather scraped off on the heel from getting caught in gratings or stepped on. The girls are chattering away, like two birds perched on a wire in the winter when the sun comes out.

"...and so he said 'you're fired'"

"Oh My God, he fired Cami?"

"She came out crying and everything. Grabbed her stuff at her desk while that witch Melissa oversaw her."

"Melissa oversaw it? Why not security?"

"Well you know Melissa, she might just be his

executive assistant, but she thinks she runs the whole office. Anyway I think they only bring in security if there is a stealing issue or something."

"Well what happened?"

"Well obviously Cami couldn't tell us, but after they had escorted her out, Melissa called all of us admin assistants together and said that John was very unhappy with the sloppiness of our administrative procedures, and the final straw had been Cami putting a post it note on his desk with a message."

"You are fucking kidding me. Had they even told you not to use post its?"

"No, that's the thing. But no one said anything. Melissa said she was going to send around a detailed procedure sheet after consultation with John, and then we would be tested on our knowledge of office procedure. If we don't do well, they are going to have to let us go."

"Is that even legal?"

"Well its not like there's a union or anything." Both girls were silent for a minute, then the one girl said "I'd quit, I hate that office, but in this economy who has a fucking choice."

As the train pulled into the station before her stop Julie looked out the window. She felt like she was caught in the grind of the brakes, that she was stuck to the seat from decades of other commuter's sweat, that she would see herself waiting on the platform for the train going in the opposite way, on her way to another temp job. Instead, she saw the man from the day before at Marv and Harv's. She sat up and stared. He was across the tracks on the other platform. He was looking right at her, smiling that black and white grin, his tie gold today, his suit charcoal grey, but his white collar shone like a beacon. *That's weird,* Julie thought *he doesn't seem like the type who would take public transit. He must get his shirts laundered, how else do they get the collar so white.* The train pulled away and Julie turned in her seat to watch the platform recede. He was still watching her, grinning, standing stock still as the other riders milled around him, blurring into nothing but a wash of dull colour.

The day drags, she's almost finished, halfway through the last week. Then it's on to the next temp job, the next periphery of an office.

At lunchtime she walks underground for a bit. She looks in the store windows, the perpetual display of things, that always illicit a low level hum of want in the back of her head. She stops beside a display for Thomas Pink shirts. It's an English brand, so the shirts are in bright colours, checks and stripes, with ties that coordinate-clash in equally bright hues. The displays are headless and she puts Dick Marvell's head on one, *no it doesn't work*, then she arranges the white collar man on the form and for a minute he is there in the case grinning at her, his mouth opening wide. She sees the reflection of the homeless girl in the glass; she's sitting against the wall behind Julie. The girl stands up and starts to come towards her, her hand is out as if she is begging, but she is grinning like the white-collar man. For just a moment their faces meld in the glass and Julie turns around, banging against the glass as she does. There is no one there except for some girls clutching Starbucks in their hands and glancing at her as they hurry past, their worn heels clacking on the tile floors. Julie is trembling. *When will this day be over, when will this be over.*

Friday, the reprieve. The last day, the weekend and then the relief of no work. For a while anyway, until the worry starts, that their will be no more temp jobs, that there will be no more jobs period, that she is useless and should have stayed in school, should have been an accountant, a teacher. But today it is the euphoria of getting free that fills Julie as she walks to work underground.

As she turns the corner by MMMuffins she sees yellow police tape roping off an area of the floor. Lying on the ground between La Senza and the muffin kiosk is something covered in a pink sheet. Julie walks around it on the La Senza side, past the pushup bras and fleece pajamas with peace symbols on them. A cop is standing by the pink mound, his face expressionless. A foot is peeking out from under the fabric, only a foot. It is wearing a brogue. A highly polished black brogue. Julie notices that the sole is leather, very little worn.

She is seeing a dead man, a dead man here on the path. She stops, unable to move, fascinated by the shoe, by the pink sheet, *had someone from La Senza brought it out? When did he die, how long has he been here?* She looks up, hoping no one will think she is gawking, a morbid death starer, and the man in the white collar is there. He is just kitty corner from her, near the MMMuffins, and he is watching her. If they stretched they could touch hands across the corner of the police tape. At this thought Julie bunches her hands into fists in her pockets. He smiles at her, not a toothy grin but with lips compressed, sliding across his face like the slow heave of a snail, and winks. She hurries away, she would run if she dared, but that would give the game away, then he would know. *Know what? That I'm scared.* She slows down in the corridor near the escalator for Marv and Harv. Two young guys in business suits walk ahead of her, clutching coffee cups and brief cases. Their shining hair is swept back, and just touches the edge of their white collars.

"Did you see that dead guy?" The one guy leans close to the other, like he is about to kiss the other man.

The other man giggles. "I know, it's always so creepy down here."

Julie takes the escalator up to the offices, hearing the clack of their shiny brogues as they walk away.

The office is dead. Not even Camilla comes in to make a latte. There is a staff Halloween party for all the Marv and Harv employees on the fifth floor. Julie sits at the computer and listens to the elevator going up and down. It's a costume party, so occasionally she see through the glass reception area doors a twenties flapper, Darth Vader, the Devil chasing Little Red Riding Hood. She knows they are sneaking into the empty offices, they look around before they go in, like naughty school children, holding hands, laughing. Julie plays Mah Jongg. For the first time all week she removes all the tiles and the dragon appears on the screen, smoke issues from his nose and **Congratulations, you win!** flashes over and over until Julie hits reset.

The man in the white-collar steps off the elevator, he is whispering in the ear of a girl, one of the girls from the train. Julie darts behind one of the chairs in reception, she crouches there, knowing he is looking for her. After a minute she creeps around the edge of the chair. The man is not there. Julie stands, she has to use the bathroom, but there's no time; she grabs her purse off the ground beneath the glass shelf, and runs to the coat closet. She struggles into her coat and boots. Forgetting all closing procedures she races for the elevators. *Come on come on come on.*

The elevator seems to stop on every floor. Julie hears voices coming from the offices near her. A man's voice, seductive. The door opens and Julie jumps in the elevator, she pushes the ground button and hits the door close button over and over again. The man in the white collar is standing there, the doors begin to shut, he tries to get a hand between them, but it is too late, just that little bit too late, and they shut and the elevator goes down.

Julie pushed herself into the corner of the elevator, but it was mirrored and her own frightened reflection cornered her every time she looked around.

Tonight she wouldn't take the path. The thought of being trapped below all the weight of these buildings, these offices filled with desks and computers and people hunched over them, What if they all collapsed and crushed those that walk below? She hurries along the sidewalks, the bright store windows offering her no comfort, the lights of cars driving past on their way home made her wish she drove, again questioning her choices, her life, because she was out and they were in. She looked behind her and thought she saw the gleam of a collar, his sharp profile reflected in a window. She began to jog. A homeless couple huddled in the doorway of a building. The woman raised her face to Julie as she passed and it was the homeless girl.

"Spare any change lady? Got any change" The girl smiles a toothless smile, obsequious and aggressive.

The man sitting next to the girl comes out of the shadows among the filthy blanket the two of them share, and it is the man in the white collar and he extends a hand, the white cuff shot, the nails manicured, the fleshy white palm unfurling towards her like a sea anemone opening to eat. Julie screams and begins to run. She looks up to see the street signs, where is she, she doesn't know anymore, and she sees him standing in the window of the nearest office building looking down at her. His hair gleams, his white shirt like a star, a bright light, his silk tie unfurling like a tongue. She looks up further and there he is again. Spinning she looks behind her and he is there, in every window in every office, filling the space between street and sky, and it seems as if each white collar man is singular and sharp, and they are all looking at her and smiling.

    Julie starts to run again and loses herself among the crowd heading down the lighted stairs to the subway, scrambling into the hot breath of the underground wafting up into the cold night air.

Beverley Wicks
TUNNELS

Waiting for the bus,
last breath of fresh air,
boarding with crowds,
showered fresh for the day.

Roars into the station,
tossed up like a salad,
past turnstiles spinning,
race onto the stairs.

Subway roars to a stop,
drenching with dust bits,
doors rolling open,
compression moves deeper.

Jolting onward to work,
wiggling like jelly,
rolls onto the track,
slices between reading.

Switching from platforms,
pressing forward, foul air,
roll on to downtown,
released to the buildings.

Standing, waiting to breathe,
crowds walk unreleased,
into corridors of boutiques,
rushing forward to missions.

Levitating elevator upwards,
for the accomplished to work,
southern Toronto views,
a pane of clear glass.

CONTRIBUTORS

Martha Baillie is the author of four novels—in three of them a suicide occurs (a dark recommendation at best). Extended exposure to conceptual art has occasionally compelled Martha to roll cigarettes from the pages of her novels, to drill and extract core samples from her manuscripts, and to apply acupuncture needles to her prose, in the hope of improving narrative flow. Martha is a bilingual storyteller and has been a white collar employee of the Toronto Public Library for over twenty years. Her most recent novel, *The Incident Report* (Pedlar Press) is comprised of 144 fragments and set in an inner city library, home to the mad and the marginalized. It was nominated for the Scotiabank Giller Prize and chosen by the *Globe & Mail* as a Best Book for 2009.

Brian Bartlett of Halifax has published many books of poems, including *Wanting the Day: Selected Poems* (Atlantic Poetry Prize 2004) and *The Watchmaker's Table* (Acorn-Plantos People's Poetry Award 2009). The most recent of his four chapbooks, *Being Charlie*, is a haiku-montage inspired by the films of Charlie Chaplin. He has also edited a book of prose, *Don McKay: Essays on His Works*, and three volumes of selected poems: *Earthly Pages: The Poetry of Don Domanski*, *The Essential James Reaney*, and, forthcoming in spring 2012, *The Essential Robert Gibbs*. Since 1990 he has taught Creative Writing and various fields of literature at Saint Mary's University.

Conrad Black, author, historian, biographer, Canadian man of letters, and former head of Argus and Hollinger corporate groups and of London's *Telegraph* newspapers, is founder of *The National Post*. He has authored the critically acclaimed biographies of Maurice Duplessis, Franklin Roosevelt and Richard Nixon. His most recent book is *A Matter of Principle*.

Marilyn Bowering has received many awards for her writing (both poetry and fiction) including the Pat Lowther Award, the Dorothy Livesay Prize and several National Magazine awards. Her work has been shortlisted for the Governor General's Prize and for significant international awards including the Dublin Impac Award, the Orange Prize, the Sony Award and the Prix Italia. She was a 2008 Fulbright Scholar at New York University and currently teaches at Vancouver Island

University. Her most recent books are *Green* (poetry) and *What It Takes To Be Human* (novel). Marilyn Bowering lives in Sooke, B.C.

April Bulmer has had six books of poetry published. Her most recent collection is called *The Goddess Psalms* (Serengeti Press). Her work often promotes the world of women and spirituality as she holds Masters Degrees in Creative Writing, Religious Studies and Theological Studies. Her poetry has appeared in *the Malahat Review, Arc, The Anglican Theological Review,* Harvard University's *Journal of Feminist Studies in Religion*, and *the Globe and Mail*, to name a few publications. New poems will appear in an upcoming issue of *the Windsor Review*. Her white collar work has included years at TVOntario and *Maclean's* magazine. She is originally from Toronto, but now lives in the small southwestern Ontario city of Cambridge where she writes regularly and cares for her dog, Lichee.

Barry Callaghan, the well-known novelist, poet, and man of letters, is included in every major Canadian anthology and his fiction and poetry have been translated into seven languages. His works include *The Hogg Poems and Drawings* (1978), *The Black Queen*

Stories (1982), *The Way The Angel Spreads Her Wings* (1989). *When Things Get Worst* (1993), *A Kiss Is Still A Kiss* (1995), *Hogg, The Poems And Drawings* (1997), *Barrelhouse Kings: A Memoir* (1998), *Hogg: The Seven Last Words* (2001), *Raise You Five: Essays and Encounters 1964-2004, Volume One* (2005). *Raise You Ten: Essays and Encounters 1964-2004, Volume Two* (2006), *Between Trains* (2007), *Beside Still Waters* (2009), *Raise You Twenty: Essays and Encounters 1964-2011, Volume Three* (2011). He has published translations of French, Serbian, and Latvian poetry, and has been writer in-residence at the universities of Rome, Venice, Bologna, and Mexico City. He was a war correspondent in the Middle East and Africa in the 70s, at the same time began the internationally celebrated quarterly and press, *Exile* and Exile Editions. *Exile* is in its 34th Volume and as editor he has overseen the publication of more than 1000 writers.

James Clarke is a retired judge of the Superior Court of Ontario. He is author of eight collections of poetry plus two prose books. He lives in Guelph, Ontario where he is presently at work on a childhood memoir of the war years.

Brian Campbell's most recent collection is *Passenger Flight* (Signature, 2009). He is also the author of *Guatemala and Other Poems* (1994) and *Undressing the Night* (2007), a translation of selected work of the Nicaraguan-Canadian poet, Francisco Santos. Brian's poetry has appeared in numerous reviews, including *CV2*, *The New Quarterly*, *Prairie Fire,* and *The Saranac Review*; it was also shortlisted for the 2006 CBC Literary Awards. Brian writes book reviews for *The Rover* and the *Montreal Review of Books*. He lives and teaches in Montreal, and thankfully, has spent comparatively little time in offices where white collar work is done.

Sue Chenette is a poet and classical pianist who grew up in northern Wisconsin and has made her home in Toronto since 1972. She is the author of three chapbooks: *A Transport of Grief*, *Solitude in Cloud and Sun*, and *The Time Between Us*, which won the Canadian Poetry Association's Shaunt Basmajian Award in 2001. Her full-length collection *Slender Human Weight* was published by Guernica Editions in 2009, and her second collection, *The Bones of His Being*, will be released by Guernica early in 2012.

Brandon Crilly is currently pursuing a Bachelor of Education at Queen's University. He hopes to teach high school History and English (job market providing, of course) and to never find himself in "the black room." His short fiction has appeared in *CommuterLit*, *Ultraviolet*, and *529: An Anthology*, edited by Stuart Ross. He would like to thank Carolyn Smart for her insight into this piece, and as always his partner Amber Vincze, simply for being there.

Cyril Dabydeen's recent book of poetry is *Unanimous Night* (Black Moss Press). A former Poet Laureate of Ottawa, his work has appeared internationally, including in the Oxford, Penguin, and Heinemann Books of Caribbean Verse. His novel *Drums Of My Flesh* (TSAR Publications) won the Guyana Prize for Best Book of Fiction and was nominated for the IMPAC/Dublin Literary Prize. He has edited *Beyond Sangre Grande: Caribbean Writing Today* (TSAR), *A Shapely Fire: Changing the Literary Landscape* (Mosaic Press), and *Another Way To Dance: Contemporary Asian Poetry From Canada and the United States* (TSAR). He lives in Ottawa.

Carlinda D'Alimonte teaches English and Creative Writing at an arts-based high school in Windsor, Ontario where she is Department Head of English. She regularly organizes readings and clinics given by visiting writers and has co-authored several online English courses, including Grade 12 Writer's Craft. She has authored two books of poetry published by Black Moss Press—*Now That We Know Who We Are* (2004), and *Other Living Things* (2009). Her works have appeared in several anthologies and literary magazines. She holds both Canadian and Italian citizenship and lives in Tecumseh, Ontario.

Christopher Doda is a poet, editor and critic living in Toronto. He is the author of two books of poetry, *Among Ruins* and *Aesthetics Lesson*, both from Mansfield Press. He is also the Series Editor for *Best Canadian Essays* and the review editor for the online journal *Studio*.

Paula Eisenstein is a Toronto area writer who continues to work by day in a government call center. She is a member of the Influency Salon editorial group. She obtained a BA in English from Mt. Allison University.

Jesse Patrick Ferguson has lived in Cornwall, Ottawa, Fredericton, and Sydney, Cape Breton. He has published poetry and reviews in ten countries, in both print and online formats. Some highlights include: *Canadian Literature*, *Prairie Fire*, *The Walrus*, *Poetry Ireland Review*, *Poetry* and *Harper's*. His work also appears in the anthologies *Best Canadian Poetry, 2009* and *Rogue Stimulus*. Jesse has been a poetry editor for *The Fiddlehead*, and he has served on the editorial boards of several other Canadian journals. In 2009, Freehand Books published his first full-length poetry collection, *Harmonics*.

Marty Gervais is an award-winning journalist, poet, playwright, historian, photographer and editor. As a writer, he has written more than a dozen books of poetry, two plays, and a novel. His most successful work, *The Rumrunners*, a book about the Prohibition period, was a Canadian bestseller.

Steven Heighton's most recent books are *Workbook: memos & dispatches on writing* and the novel *Every Lost Country*. His 2005 novel, *Afterlands*, appeared in six countries; was a *New York Times Book Review* editors' choice; was a best of year choice in ten publications in Canada, the USA, and the UK; and has been optioned for film. His poems and stories have appeared in many publications—including *London Review of Books*, *Poet-*

ry, *Tin House, The Walrus,* and *Best English Stories*—and have received four gold National Magazine Awards. He has also been nominated for the Governor General's Award and Britain's W.H. Smith Award. In 2012 Knopf Canada will publish *The Dead Are More Visible*, a collection of short stories including "Noughts & Crosses."

Bill Howell has five poetry collections, most recently *Porcupine Archery* (Insomniac Press). One of his favourite targets is corporate greed culture, which refuses to distinguish between marketing and art. Bill was a network producer-director with CBC Radio Drama for three decades, until a new regime decided "to go another way." Unloved by hardcore Tories everywhere, Howell remains in Toronto.

A.M. Klein (1909-1972) was a poet, novelist, and journalist as well as a leading figure in Jewish-Canadian culture and proponent of literary modernism in Canada. Born in Ratno, Ukraine, he moved at the age of three to Montreal, the city where he would live most of his life. He is perhaps best-known for his Governor General's Award-winning collection *The Rocking Chair and other poems* (1948) and for his novella, *The Second Scroll* (1951). A lawyer by profession, he was speech writer for industrialist Samuel Bronfman and, from 1932-1955, the editor the Canadian Jewish Chronicle. His literary legacy is honoured through the A.M. Klein Prize for Poetry awarded by the Quebec Writers' Federation.

Stephen Leacock (1869-1944) was the acclaimed Canadian humorist, educator and economist who is best remembered for his book *Sunshine Sketches of a Little Town* (1912). "My Financial Career" appeared in Leacock's *Literary Lapses* (1910). He taught at McGill University, but is best remembered for his association with the city of Orillia, Ontario, where his summer home remains one of the city's principal tourist attractions.

John B. Lee is Poet Laureate of Brantford and Poet Laureate of Norfolk County. His work has appeared internationally in over 500 publications. The most recent of his books include: *Dressed in Dead Uncles*, (Black Moss Press, 2010); *In the Muddy Shoes of Morning*, (Hidden Brook Press, 2011); and *King Joe: A Matter of Treason—the Life and Times of Joseph Willcocks*, (Heronwood Enterprises, 2011).

Seymour Mayne is the author, editor or translator of more than fifty books and monographs. His latest collections include *September Rain* 2005, *Les pluies de septembre* 2008 (his selected poems translated into French), *Reflejos: Sonetos de una palabra* 2008 (a bilingual Spanish edition of his selected word sonnets), *Fly Off into the Strongest Light* 2009 (his selected poems translated into Hebrew), and *Ricochet: Word Sonnets/Sonnets d'un mot* 2011 (a bilingual French edition of his word sonnets). A fervent innovator of the word sonnet, he has given readings and lectured widely in Canada and abroad on this unique new miniature form. He serves as Professor of Canadian Literature, Canadian Studies, and Creative Writing at the University of Ottawa.

Shane Neilson is a family physician whose poetry volumes include *Exterminate My Heart*, *Meniscus*, *Complete Physical*, and *Alice and George*. He has also published a memoir about his training as a physician titled *Call Me Doctor*. His work has also been anthologized in *The New Canon*, *In Fine Form*, and he edited *Alden Nowlan and Illness*. The poem "No Ill Effects" appears in this volume by permission of Porcupine's Quill Press.

John Oughton is Professor of Learning and Teaching at Centennial College, and the author of five books of poetry, most recently *Time Slip* from Guernica Editions He has written over 400 articles, interviews, reviews and blogs, and is also a photographer. Previously, he worked in corporate communications and audio-visual.

P.K. Page (1916-2010) published over thirty books of poetry, fiction, non-fiction, and children's literature during a career that spanned more than seven decades. She won the Governor General's Award for Poetry in 1954 and 1985, and was a fellow of the Royal Society of Canada. She was one of Canada's leading Modernist voices.

Molly Peacock, a poet and creative nonfiction writer, is the author of *The Paper Garden: Mrs. Delany Begins Her Life's Work at 72* (McClelland and Stewart, 2010; Bloomsbury, 2011) and six books of poetry, including *The Second Blush* (W. W. Norton and Company, 2008; McClelland and Stewart, 2009) and *Cornucopia: New & Selected Poems* (W. W. Norton and Company in US and UK and Penguin Canada, 2002). Among her other works are a memoir called *Paradise, Piece By Piece* and *How to Read a Poem and Start a Poetry Circle* (1998, 1999; both published by Riverhead Penguin in the US and McClelland and Stewart in Canada). She also serves as Series Editor of *The Best Canadian Poetry* (Tightrope Books).

Lauralee Proudfoot, after more than 20 years working in a variety of social services capacities, returned to school in 1998. Since completing the Computer Programmer Analyst diploma at Georgian College in Barrie, she has taught various computer applications. She also earned a BA in English Literature from Laurentian University and an MA in English (Public Texts) from Trent University in Peterborough, where she is now working toward a PhD in Canadian Studies. In her free time, she provides technical support to her husband's home-based business, enjoys her puppies, fishing and online games, and writes poetry and fiction.

Julie Roorda is the author of three volumes of poetry *Eleventh Toe* (2001), *Courage Underground* (2006), and most recently *Floating Bodies* (2010), all published by Guernica Editions. She has also published a collection of short stories called *Naked in the Sanctuary* (Guernica Editions, 2004) and a novel for young adults *Wings of a Bee* (2007) published by Sumach Press. She lives in Toronto.

Robert Service (1874-1958) was the author of twenty three books of poetry and fiction, the most notable of which include *Songs of a Sourdough* (1907), *Ballads of a Cheechako* (1909), *Rhymes of a Rolling Stone* (1912), and *Rhymes of a Red Cross Man* (1916). He is best remembered for his iconic poems about the Yukon Gold Rush including "The Shooting of Dan McGrew" and "The Cremation of Sam McGee."

Adam Sol had a brief but educational life in the corporate sector, for which he is still doing penance. He is the author of three books of poetry, including *Jeremiah, Ohio*, a novel in poems which was shortlisted for Ontario's Trillium Award for Poetry; and *Crowd of Sounds*, which won the award in 2004. He teaches at Laurentian University's campus in Barrie, Ontario, and lives in Toronto with his wife and three sons.

Raymond Souster has published more than fifty volumes of poetry during his lengthy career as a poet and mentor, including the most recent volumes *Rags, Bones and Bottles* and *Big Smoke Blues* and his ten volume *Collected Poems*. Currently in his ninetieth year, he continues to write and publish. One of the founders of the League of Canadian Poets, *Contact* magazine and Contact Press, he has won the Governor General's Award for Poetry (1964) and the City of Toronto Book Award (1980). He lives in Toronto.

Robert Sward has taught at Cornell University, the Iowa Writers' Workshop and UC Santa Cruz. A Guggenheim Fellow, he was chosen by Lucile Clifton to receive a Villa Montalvo Literary Arts Award. His more than 20 books include: *Four Incarnations* (Coffee House Press), *Rosicrucian in the Basement*, *The Collected Poems*, and *God is in the Cracks* (Black Moss Press, Canada), now in its second printing. His latest, *New & Selected Poems, 1957-2011*, is being published by Red Hen Press.

George Swede has published 35 collections of poetry (20 chapbooks and 15 perfect bound volumes) with publishers in Canada, the United States and the United Kingdom. His two latest were published by Edmonton's Inkling Press in 2010: *Joy In Me Still* (haiku) and *White Thoughts, Blue Mind* (tanka). In 1977, he co-founded Haiku Canada and for 2008-09, he was the Honourary Curator of the American Haiku Archives at the California State Library in Sacramento. Since 2008, he has been the first Canadian editor of *Frogpond: Journal of the Haiku Society of America*.

H. Masud Taj is an oral poet, calligrapher, and architect who composes poems in his head and leaves them there. His downloaded poems have been featured in anthologies of Indian poets (*Penguin Books* India 2002; *Wespennest* Austria 2006; *Bloodaxe* UK 2008; *TLR* USA 2009) as well as Canadian poets (*Atlas* 2007; *Rogue Stimulus* 2010), and are archived in the *Special Poetry Collection* of Carleton University, where he is Adjunct Professor of Architecture. He was nominated for the best lecturer in TV Ontario's *Big Ideas* series in 2005 and is winner of the Capital Educator's Award for 2011. He lives with his family in Ottawa.

Priscila Uppal is a Toronto poet, fiction writer and York University professor. Among her publications are eight collections of poetry, most recently, *Ontological Necessities* (2006; shortlisted for the $50,000 Griffin Poetry Prize), *Traumatology* (2010), *Successful Tragedies: Poems 1998-2010* (Bloodaxe Books, U.K.), and *Winter Sport: Poems* (2010); the critically-acclaimed novels *The Divine Economy of Salvation* (2002) and *To Whom It May Concern* (2009); and the study *We Are What We Mourn: The Contemporary English-Canadian Elegy* (2009). She is on the Board of Directors at the Toronto Arts Council, and was poet-in-residence for Canadian Athletes Now during the 2010 Vancouver Olympic and Paralympic games. *Time Out London* recently dubbed her "Canada's coolest poet."

Halli Villegas is the author of three collections of poetry (*Red Promises, In the Silence Absence Makes,* and *The Human Cannonball*), a book of ghost stories (*The Hairwreath and Other Stories*) and several anthology pieces, including pieces in text books for reluctant readers. She has received funding for her writing through grants from the Ontario Arts Council and the Toronto Arts Council.

Beverley Wicks was born in Toronto and grew up in Etobicoke. She is a graduate of OISE of the University of Toronto, Laurentian University at Georgian College in Barrie, and Conestoga College in Kitchener. Beverley is the winner of the Dennie Prize for Prose and was a finalist for the Gordon Prize for Poetry. She writes short stories and poetry, and is currently writing a novel. Beverley lives in Barrie, Ontario with her family and is working on her Master of Education at Nipissing University.

THE EDITORS

Bruce Meyer is author of thirty-two books of poetry, short fiction, non-fiction and pedagogy including the national bestseller, *The Golden Thread: A Reader's Journey Through the Great Books*. His most recent volumes of poetry are *Mesopotamia* (2010), and *Dog Days: A Comedy of Terriers* (2010). His most recent book is *Alphabestiary: An Emblem Book* with H. Masud Taj. His broadcasts on literature for CBC Radio One (*The Great Books*, *A Novel Idea*, and *Great Poetry*) with Michael Enright are the network's bestselling spoken word CD series. He is the inaugural Poet Laureate for the City of Barrie and professor of English at Georgian College.

Carolyn Meyer is a tenured Assistant Professor and business communication researcher in the School of Professional Communication and the Master of Professional Communication Program at Ryerson University (Toronto, Canada). She is the co-author of *The Reader: Contemporary Essays and Writing Strategies* (Prentice Hall Canada, 2001) and the author of *Communicating for Results: A Canadian Student's Guide*, 2nd ed., (Oxford University Press, 2010), a guide to professional writing first published in 2007 and now used at over 20 colleges and universities across Canada. She is currently the Vice-President (Canada) of the Association for Business Communication. Her literary criticism has been published in *Agenda* (UK) and *The Dictionary of Literary Biography*.

ACKNOWLEDGMENTS

Many thanks are owed to Conrad Black, James Deahl, Donna Dunlop, Beth Follet, Elke Inkster, Tim Inkster, Seymour Mayne, Raymond Souster, Joan Maida, Brian Fox, Margaret Meyer, Karen Monck, Barry Callaghan, and Kate Hargreaves.

Martha's Baillie's excerpts from *The Incident* (Pedlar Press, 2009) appears by permission of the author and Pedlar Press; Brian Bartlett's "Foot Doctor for the Homeless" and "The Sonographer" appeared in *The Afterlife Tree* and are published here by permission of the author and McGill Queen's University Press; Barry Callaghan's "Mellow Yellow" appeared in *A Kiss Is Still A Kiss and other stories* (Little Brown and Company, 1995) and appears here by permission of the author; A.M. Klein's "Annual Banquet: Chambre de Commerce" appears by permission of the Estate of A.M. Klein and University of Toronto Press; Stephen Leacock's "My Financial Career" appeared originally in *Literary Lapses* (1910); Bruce Meyer's "Success" appeared in *The Presence* (1997) and is published here by permission of the author and Black Moss Press; "Death and the Human Resources Manager," appeared in *Anywhere* published by Exile Editions and is reprinted here by permission of the author and Exile Editions; Shane Neilson's "No Ill Effects" appeared in *Complete Physical* (2010) and is published here courtesy of the author and Porcupine's Quill Press; P.K. Page's "The Stenographers" appears by permission of Porcupine's Quill Press; Molly Peacock's "Our Room" appeared in *Raw Heaven* and is reprinted here by permission of the author and W.W. Norton and Company, New York; Raymond Souster's "This Day" appeared in *Big Smoke Blues* (2010) and is published here by permission of the author.

FOR MORE CONTENT
VISIT BLACK MOSS PRESS
ONLINE AT
WWW.BLACKMOSSPRESS.COM

Québec, Canada
2011

Printed on Silva Enviro 100% post-consumer EcoLogo certified paper, processed chlorine free and manufactured using biogas energy.